DATE DUE

DEMCO 38-296

Shakespeare's Criminals

Recent Titles in
Contributions in Criminology and Penology

SHAKESPEARE'S CRIMINALS

Criminology, Fiction, and Drama

VICTORIA M. TIME

Contributions in Criminology and Penology, Number 52

GREENWOOD PRESS
Westport, Connecticut • London

Library of Congress Cataloging-in-Publication Data

Time, Victoria M., 1962–
    Shakespeare's criminals : criminology, fiction, and drama /
Victoria M. Time.
      p. cm.—(Contributions in criminology and penology, ISSN
0732–4464 ; no. 52)
    Includes bibliographical references and index.
    ISBN 0–313–30870–5 (alk. paper)
    1. Shakespeare, William, 1564–1616—Characters—Criminals.
2. Criminology—England—History—16th century. 3. Criminology—
England—History—17th century. 4. Crime—England—History—16th
century. 5. Crime—England—History—17th century. 6. Criminals in
literature. 7. Crime in literature. I. Title. II. Series.
PR3026.T55 1999
822.3'3—dc21   99–22098

British Library Cataloguing in Publication Data is available.

Library of Congress Catalog Card Number: 99–22098
ISBN: 0–313–30870–5
ISSN: 0732–4464

First published in 1999

Greenwood Press, 88 Post Road West, Westport, CT 06881
An imprint of Greenwood Publishing Group, Inc.
www.greenwood.com

Printed in the United States of America

The paper used in this book complies with the
Permanent Paper Standard issued by the National
Information Standards Organization (Z39.48–1984).

10 9 8 7 6 5 4 3 2 1

To my parents, Maria and John Time

Contents

Preface

This volume explores how William Shakespeare used the themes of law and justice in his plays and how his writing presents theatrical scenarios directly relevant to historical as well as contemporary criminological thinking.

Shakespeare lived over 400 years ago, before criminological theory was formalized and long before criminology emerged as an academic discipline. Yet, arguably, his works are timeless and of relevance across geographical boundaries.

Three categories of research questions form the basis of the book. First, from a purely descriptive perspective, in what ways does Shakespeare use dramatic characters in his plays to illustrate criminal or deviant behavior? Specifically, what crimes are depicted in selected plays and how are they defined and portrayed? Second, how do Shakespeare's characters or story lines illustrate motivations for criminal behavior? That is, how do Shakespeare's works explain the existence of crime and criminal careers in society? How does the playwright discuss or allude to biological or personality variables influencing criminal conduct? How does he develop the ideas of sociocultural and economic impact on crime? In these regards, do his theatrical scenarios concerning criminality and crime causation appear to anticipate or foreshadow the criminological theory that has appeared in the subsequent professional literature hundreds of years later? Third, how do Shakespearean plays offer explanation and analogies for various models of social control? For instance, does he offer any suggestions for crime prevention, legal and judicial procedures, and correctional sanctions?

Six Shakespearean plays purposefully selected from the genres of comedy, tragedy, and history are analyzed here. Two plays represent each genre: *Measure for Measure* and *The Merchant of Venice*, comedy; *Othello* and *Macbeth*, tragedy; *Richard III* and *1 Henry IV*, history. Occasionally, other plays are introduced to augment the original sample of six plays.

Citations of a literary genius such as Shakespeare rarely appear in modern criminological treaties. By filling this void, this book will open novel theoretical avenues for conceptualizing the issues of crime and justice.

Part I states the problem and sets Shakespeare's writings in a historical concept. The premise is that the discipline of criminology should broaden its search for answers as to why people commit crimes. Literary works have seldom been reviewed for insights even though literary writers from time immemorial have been writing about crime and criminals. This part also summarizes the problems that plagued England during Shakespeare's time.

Part II focuses on the crimes and deviance engaged in by selected characters in the sample plays. The crimes are discussed under three main categories: violence against the person, property crimes, noncriminal deviance and nonviolent sexual deviance.

In Part III, the crux of the book, the relationship between criminological theory and the behavior of selected Shakespearean characters is examined. Twelve main criminological theories or perspectives are discussed.

The analysis in Part IV concentrates on social control and legal issues. Here, the various types of social control Shakespeare advocated are discussed. In addition, other issues raised in the plays, such as deterrence and judicial ethics, are considered.

All citations are from *The Complete Works of William Shakespeare: Thirty-Seven Volumes in One* (New York: Walter J. Black, Inc., n.d.).

Acknowledgments

I am indebted to Drs. W. Timothy Austin and Ronald G. Shafer of Indiana University of Pennsylvania, for their guidance, their kind words of encouragement and support, and their interest in this book and in my budding career. I am profoundly grateful to them.

I would also like to thank Mrs. Isabelle Foster and Morgan Reade for their many kindnesses to me and Reverend and Mrs. Frederick and Dr. Concetta Culliver for their prayers and good wishes. My gratitude is also extended to Dennis Shepherd and Louis Mizell, Jr. for their countless favors. To all my friends whose names I withhold to avoid inadvertent omission of some: thank you for being there for me.

I also thank Dr. Heather Ruland Staines, Rebecca Ardwin, and all the other editors at Greenwood Publishing Group for believing in the worth of this volume and for their various roles in its production.

Finally, I wish to record my words of infinite gratitude to my parents, Maria and John Time, for the good life they gave me and, in particular, for all the sacrifices and investments they made toward my education.

PART I

THE PROBLEM AND ELIZABETHAN ENGLAND

1
A Case for the Use of Literary Works in Criminology

In the latter part of the nineteenth century, many works on crime were published as sociological treatises because the discipline of criminology had not yet been formalized. Fictional works were an important early source of publications on crime and criminals. Unfortunately, fiction writers, who wrote about crime centuries before such theorists as Cesare Beccaria, Jeremy Bentham, and Cesare Lombroso, seldom have been cited in modern criminological or other social science treatises even though fiction writers arguably have provided significant theoretical discussions of crime and justice issues. Several disciplines are complementary to criminology, but none alone can make the criminal phenomenon clear. Biology, psychology, and sociology, for instance, explain criminal etiology; criminal law addresses penology and correction. The great works of literature can make a significant contribution to the study of criminal psychology.

One of the earliest to conceptualize crime in fictional writings was William Shakespeare.

Although Shakespeare is acclaimed as a genius in poetry and drama, the Bard has seldom been considered a criminological theorist. Through some of the fictional characters in his plays, Shakespeare, in several subtle and apparent ways, explored the reasons that motivated some to crime and deviance. These theories, propounded by Shakespeare more than 350 years ago, are rarely featured in textbooks on criminology, cited in professional journals, or considered in research reports. H. Mannheim

(1967) and S. Schafer (1969) comprise the few scholarly sources in criminology that recognize Shakespeare's insights.

Shakespeare's works have been the subject of many dissertations and books written by scholars in a variety of disciplines, including law, political science, sociology, history, theology, and literature, among others. Some of these studies have viewed Shakespeare as a jurist, or as a politician, and some have attempted to link Shakespeare's works with criminological thought although they wrote under different disciplinary perspectives. K. G. Pories (1995), whose specialty is literature, examines in her dissertation, entitled "Fashioning the Face of Poverty in Early Modern England," how poor people and criminals were portrayed in the sixteenth and early seventeenth centuries by "legislation," "debates in parliament," "sermons," "literature," and "canonical studies." In her analysis, Pories relies, in part, on Shakespeare's *Henry* plays and *The Taming of the Shrew*. Among the multitude of authors who have written about Shakespeare's plays, only A. Goll, in his early book *Criminal Types in Shakespeare* (1909), seems to have formed a direct nexus between Shakespeare's works and what is now included in the discipline of criminology.

Although these dissertations and books are insightful, there is still a considerable amount of theoretical work on crime and criminals in Shakespeare's writings that needs to be brought to light. This book endeavors to accomplish that task by providing a foundation on which fictional works relevant to criminology can be incorporated into conventional text material. The material in this book is by no means exhaustive of Shakespearean plays and ideas. Six plays form the basis of analysis although occasional reference is made to other plays. The intent is to use these six plays to demonstrate that ideas about human behavior can be extracted from sources that may, at first glance, appear to be unlikely ones.

SIGNIFICANCE OF THE USE OF LITERARY WORKS IN CRIMINOLOGY

For several centuries, society has struggled with crime and has continuously sought to understand the criminal mind and why or how society breeds criminal conduct.

As our readings of textbooks in criminology reveal, most of the contributions to the development of the discipline have been made by theorists and researchers with backgrounds in other disciplines. These include, for example, law, medicine, sociology, anthropology, psychology, and economics. Seldom have contributions from authors in the field of drama or literature been recognized. Long before Lombroso and more contemporary criminologists espoused their various theories of crime, fiction writers and dramatists had written volumes of literature with theatrical or fictional scenarios that addressed most historical and contemporary criminological thinking.

Schafer, for example, has made the point that, although Lombroso has been acclaimed as "the great instigator of ideas in criminology," Lombroso was certainly not the first "instigator" (1969, p. 111). Schafer cites Homer and Shakespeare, among others, as some of the early precursors in the quest to understand criminality.

The reason for the omission of literary observers is unclear. Perhaps it could be found in the notion that knowledge that delves to the roots of causality must be researched empirically among real human beings in their natural environments (see, for example, the discussion of theory and research by T. Hirschi 1969; W. Wallace 1971; G. Vold and T. Bernard 1986). One can reasonably presume Shakespeare's exclusion from most texts in criminology results from the fact that his characters are fictional. If this "scientific orientation" is the reason for the exclusion, perhaps the discipline is ignoring the point that deriving an appropriate interpretation of the facts collected through observations requires knowledge and experience of specific segments of life, which must be understood, interpreted, and assessed (see Mannheim 1967).

This is precisely the empirical genius of Shakespeare. His plays were not abstractions of fairy tales; they were reflections of the ongoing themes of society albeit some seemed embellished. By neglecting Shakespeare's characters, we omit any analysis of their human behavior, a consideration of which could provide a more comprehensive understanding of crime and justice. When we read Shakespeare's plays, we are able to follow the mind of the criminal actor and justice-oriented issues in a way we sometimes neglect to do in our own traditional social science attempts to interpret, evaluate, and understand human behavior. Some criminologists align themselves with one perspective of crime causation, whereas Shakespeare accommodated a more integrative orientation in his explanations of why some of his characters resort to crime and deviance. As a discipline with no autonomous origin, criminology is likely to make more strides by looking for ideas even where none appears likely.

E. Sagarin contends that the only difference between criminological and literary writers is "method" (1980, p. 80). He explains that criminologists come to conclusions about crime and related issues through "studies based on selected samples rather than one or several individuals" (p. 80). Sagarin argues that the samples "are or aspire to be representative; just of what and whom is not always clear" and that because there is a "claim that the work is science implies that it would be replicated and give the same results if all conditions were the same" (p. 80).

On the other hand, he asserts, "The writer or the painter has studied humanity in a unique but unsystematic manner. He has learned about the world by living in it, absorbing and illuminating its appearances and realities" (p. 80). Although this technique is also practiced by social scientists who adopt a qualitative approach, they "so often naively believe in the truth of the respondents" and they couple those truths with knowledge of prior studies and make comparative tests and "competitive theory and research" (pp. 80–81). If this method seems at "first glance to be superior" to that of a literary writer or an artist, Sagarin poses the question, "Why is it difficult to find criminologists with insights into human nature comparable to those of Shakespeare and Dostoevsky?" (p. 81). This difficulty suggests that "the superiority of one method should not concern us, for both methods in the hands of profound thinkers are necessary, each for different reasons, to yield complementary portraits and the understandings that can be derived therefrom" (p. 81). It follows that, in their endeavors to understand humanity, the criminologist obtains "a representative sample, the novelist creates a representative character" (p. 81).

F. Ferracuti and M. Wolfgang also contend that criminology "requires an integration of various fields without the dominance of a single discipline or a singular orientation" (1963, pp. 156–57). While discussing the benefits of an interdisciplinary approach in understanding criminal behavior, Sagarin comments that social scientists "stand as a bridge or an island" between "literary intellectuals and physical scientists" and are "deeply interested in and involved in the work of physicists and chemists and certainly not unaware of what writers, the literary intellectuals, are saying about the social world" (1980, p. 76). Furthermore, he states, "Criminology is part of this midway culture, and at this point it is probably true that criminologists have more to learn from the literary world than the reverse." The two disciplines are "two groups of thinkers, both looking at the same object but going their separate ways" (p. 75).

Most recently, political scientists have realized the benefit and necessity of integrating auxiliary disciplines into their programs. C. Zuckert (1996), in an article published in the *Chronicle of Higher Education*, explains why political scientists should incorporate literary fiction in their scholarly pursuits.

> By depicting the fate of their characters in specific circumstances, literary works show what kinds of people tend to rise and thrive, which fail and die, under different political regimes. For example, in a collection of essays entitled "Shakespeare's Political Pageant" . . . Pamela Jensen examines why Othello, a Moor and thus an outsider in both race and religion, is able to rise to a pre-eminent position in the commercial republic of Venice. (p. A48)

Zuckert also explains that political scientists have rejected the notion that only "factual claims could be verified." While political scientists still study interest groups, as Zuckert notes, they now also study novels because "the books we read affect—as well as reflect—the way we see the world, and thus what we do in it" (p. A48).

Another negative consequence of ignoring fictional works such as those of Shakespeare is that the criminal justice system fails to benefit from his insights especially when he tailors the different kinds of social control to fit the crime and the criminal. Support for this point of view can be found in Zuckert's article. She notes that Austin Sarat of Amherst College teaches a course on murder, and his students are required to read any one of Agatha Christie's novels, *Macbeth*, or Herman Melville's *Billy Budd*. At the end, he asks his students, "To what extent can laws protect people from violence, if the law itself depends on force?" (p. A48).

Shakespeare's plays are not only inherently interesting, but also provide numerous details of human behavior. As we read his plays, it is easy to identify with his characters. While writing his plays, Shakespeare seems to have been asking why a certain character was a certain way: what led him or her to become this way. Could something be done to make him or her behave appropriately? Does that person merit punishment? If so, what punishment is appropriate? As he answers these questions in his portrayal of the characters, we can follow the steps and understand why one person chooses to commit a particular crime and how society reacts to that criminal. These are the very questions criminologists pose today as they try to understand criminal behavior.

In an article entitled "Criminology as an Interdisciplinary Behavioral Science" (1978), C. R. Jeffrey criticizes Edwin Sutherland and the discipline of criminology for limiting the explanations of criminal behavior to social variables (p. 149). Jeffrey specifically mentions viewing criminology in relation to law, sociology, psychology, and biology in order to "bring Sutherland and criminology into the twentieth century" (p. 150). Seven years later, D. Denno (1985) comments, in her article published in *Criminology*, that "the theoretical development of multi-disciplinary explanations of crime seems to be one of the most praised concepts in criminology and, at the same time, one of the most ignored in actual research" (p. 711). B. Glaser and A. Strauss advise that, "if need be, we should be as knowledgeable about literary materials as literary critics and other men of letters; but again without abandoning special sociological purposes" (1967, p. 163).

These comments highlight the point that, since the discipline is still in the developing stages of trying to understand crime and justice, it seems naive to exclude the insights of other disciplines and some of their contributors; in this case, literature, particularly that of Shakespeare. In

Mannheim's words, "Closer scrutiny of the literature shows that not too much should be taken for granted in this field" (1967, p. 12). Echoing Jeffrey, if we consider fiction in the search for an understanding of criminal behavior, we might bring criminology into the twenty-first century.

S. Finkelstein had this to say in response to the title of his book *Who Needs Shakespeare?*:

> We all need him. . . . We need him as an artist who, writing in the early or prerevolutionary stage of capitalism, grasped that changes were under way and put foremost in his work a concern for human values. . . . He carried his concern for human values into the consideration of the central issues of the day, and in so doing encompassed in his art a range of characters from the highest strata to the lowest. He raised questions that capitalism, even with all the revolutions (which began in the 1640's, after his death), was not able to answer, and that are still on the agenda today. And now that capitalism in crisis becomes more savagely corrupt and inhuman and is being challenged by the rise of socialism, we need his humanity to illuminate these questions and to assure us that they are still central to the solutions that pave the way to human happiness. (1973, p. 24)

ISSUES

It is argued in this book that, although William Shakespeare wrote almost four hundred years ago, his ideas focus directly on issues still pertinent to contemporary criminological thought. Criminologists have systematically overlooked the relevancy of his works. This book addresses three sets of research questions based on a purposive sample of Shakespeare's plays which include themes relevant to crime and justice theory.

First, from a purely descriptive perspective, in what ways does Shakespeare use dramatic characters in his plays to illustrate criminal or deviant behavior? Specifically, what crimes are depicted in selected plays and how are they defined and portrayed? Do any patterns or broad classifications emerge? For instance, do Shakespearean plays contain more violent, property, or sexual crimes? Is criminality more prevalent in one gender than the other? Are certain types of offenders portrayed as stereotypes?

Second, how do Shakespeare's characters or story lines illustrate motivations or conditions that lead to or influence crime and criminal behavior? How do Shakespeare's works explain the existence of crime and criminal careers in society? For example, in what ways does the playwright discuss or allude to biological or personality variables that influence criminal conduct? How does he develop the ideas of sociocultural and economic impact on crime? In this regard, do his theatrical scenarios concerning criminality and crime causation appear to anticipate or foreshadow the criminological theory appearing in professional literature hundreds of years later?

Third, how do Shakespearean plays offer explanations and analogies for various models of social control? For instance, in what ways does Shakespeare offer correctional sanctions for criminal misconduct? Does he discuss individual or personal needs for control (self-control) versus external or official control? Does he anticipate the contemporary debate between informal versus formal social control?

Chapter 2 places Shakespeare and his plays in historical context. For readers unfamiliar with Shakespeare or the plays discussed in this book, the appendix addresses Shakespeare as a person and summarizes the plays.

SUMMARY

This chapter, points out the necessity for criminologists to study literary works, especially those of Shakespeare. Fiction writers from time immemorial have written about crime and the criminal phenomenon. Although their characters are depicted as fictional, they nevertheless represent real people in society. Several prominent writers in the social sciences, including M. Wolfgang, Sagarin, Mannheim, Jeffrey, and Glaser and Strauss, have stressed the relevance for sociologists and criminologists to extend their inquiry toward the understanding of human behavior to other disciplines.

Three issues form the basis for the analysis of the book: the kinds of crimes committed by some of the actors, the motivations for those crimes, and the types of social control discussed by Shakespeare.

2

The Historical Setting: Shakespeare's England

Shakespeare was born six years after Elizabeth I became queen of England (Neilson and Thorndike 1913, p. 1). At that time, England was predominantly a Catholic nation. In his lifetime, Shakespeare witnessed England change from being a Catholic country to becoming an increasingly Protestant one. The population of England at Shakespeare's birth was between 4 and 5 million people (1913, p. 3). Primarily an agricultural country, it provided its people with opportunities to amass wealth and gain an education. According to Neilson and Thorndike, "The nineteenth century which saw the industrial revolution . . . is the only period that equalled the Elizabethan period in the rapidity of its changes in ideas and in the condition of living" (p. 3). Class stratification was quite apparent, and rural landowners were reluctant to part with feudalism (Draper 1961, p. 3). Nevertheless, there were ample opportunities for anyone to obtain upward mobility.

Shakespeare's hometown of Stratford had a population of about 2,000 (Neilson and Thorndike 1913, p. 4). Its geographical location made it possible for it to assimilate the latest trends of modernization even though the big cities attracted those looking for a more upscale lifestyle. The local council was strict in its administration of regulations pertaining to "cleanliness, rebellions, profanity, and drunkenness" (Williams 1963, pp. 7–8; Neilson and Thorndike 1913, p. 4). Poor hygiene and uncouthness in both speech and lifestyle permeated the rural areas; occasionally Shakespeare wrote about the crudeness of the country culture as opposed to the civilized culture of the big towns (Draper 1961, p. 3; Neilson and Thorndike 1913, p. 4).

In 1564 the plague hit Stratford. In the summer of the same year, the river Avon rose, collapsing both ends of Clopton Bridge, causing massive destruction to the hay crop. In addition, wild fires were a nuisance in Stratford and in London (Schoenbaum 1987, p. 128).

London, at that time with a population of about 200,000 people, also suffered from filth, a poor water supply, disease, fire, and the plague (Neilson and Thorndike 1913, p. 6). Morals were decadent. According to M. Widmayer, "A strong trend towards Christianity in Shakespeare's age" led to an urgency to rid England of "fornicators, drunkards, dicers, wearers of vain apparel, and other imps of satan" (1988, p. 6). This trend toward the improvement of morals was quite evident in the Tudor and Stuart governments (p. 7). Shakespeare's *Measure for Measure* speaks to this movement for reform.

Although the look of London was ancient, it supplied the pomp and exciting scenery for which big cities are noted. London was full of royals, young lawyers and law students, church leaders, bankers, rich merchants, politicians, and other dignitaries (Neilson and Thorndike 1913, p. 8); and the business of entertainment was the trade in which to engage (1913, p. 8). Little wonder therefore why Shakespeare's plays were a big source of entertainment in England. Schoenbaum depicts London as a city in which just about every kind of activity occurred (1987, pp. 118–42). Most of the famous playwrights and poets, at that time, made their living in London, including Ben Jonson, Michael Drayton, and Christopher Marlowe. When Shakespeare moved to London, at the age of twenty, he relied on his experiences at Stratford, his God-given talent, and luck to break through the highly competitive London theater scene.

During the sixteenth century the Renaissance brought about numerous changes in England although those changes were most visible in such cities as London, not in the slower paced country (Draper 1961, p. 3). Different segments of society seemed to embrace the religious practices that reflected their own principles or beliefs. The large towns and cities increasingly turned to Puritanism; the rural areas, following the Stuarts, were predominantly Anglican or Roman Catholic (p. 3). London itself had more than 100 parish churches (Schoenbaum 1987, p. 121).

Politically, England witnessed several changes within the monarchy. Some of Shakespeare's works based on history were a true reflection of the order of government in his day—civil unrest, abdications, and regicides, as evident, for example, in *Macbeth* (Draper 1961, p. 10). As A. Leggatt has pointed out, Shakespeare is not concerned "with what political structures best serve the generalized good, but in watching how people behave within the structures they have" (1988, p. 238). Therefore, although Shakespeare lived in a politically troubled time, his views on politics were "exploratory rather than prescriptive." His ideas, according to Leggatt, "will not help us to control the economy, achieve social justice, win or prevent war. But it tells us something about human power and the endless fascination it has for us in the face of our own mortality" (1988, p. 243).

Economic progress was also stimulated by the Renaissance. The rich merchants and bankers instituted the system of "loans-at-interest," a financial practice that provided a springboard for contemporary capitalist practices (Draper 1961, p. 128). Rich merchants also copied this system in their financial and commercial transactions with other merchants. Shakespeare's *The Merchant of Venice* mirrored this period in Europe. London was a commercial center that merchants from different parts of England, the Netherlands, and other European countries found very accessible because of the navigable river Thames (see Neilson and Thorndike, pp. 3, 6). Migration into the big towns and cities was widespread. Refugees fleeing from religious persecution in France and the Netherlands moved to London (Schoenbaum 1987, p. 126). London soon experienced great heterogeneity and population mobility.

Although court records at the time do not indicate a proliferation of white-collar crime, there are documented instances of unfair trade practices. Forgery, embezzlement, uttering, and false pretense were the white-collar crimes that sprang out of increasing commerce. In 1563 first-time forgery of some kinds of deeds and documents, particularly those pertaining to real estate, was classified as a misdemeanor. The offense was upgraded to a felony upon a second occurrence (Sharpe 1984, p. 177). In the 1700s a series of legislation classified all types of forgery as felonies, but records do not indicate that forgery was a prevalent crime.

Although London attracted many fortune seekers, the dangers of living in or commuting to the city were obvious. The risks of being attacked by highwaymen exceeded the discomforts of traveling on the bad roads (Rolfe 1904, p. 119). Traveling alone or unarmed was a very unsafe venture; however, traveling armed, or with company, was no guarantee of safety because armed robbers had far more dangerous weapons. Rolfe (1904, quoting Harrison, n.d.) notes that, in Shakespeare's day, chamberlains, tapsters, and hostlers of inns were informants of robbers, and supports his assertion by citing Shakespeare's *1 Henry IV* (II.i.54–56). In the play, Gadshill says to the chamberlain in the inn at Rochester, "Thou variest no more from picking of purses, than giving direction doth from labouring; thou lay'st the plot, how." The chamberlain then discloses to Gadshill which guests in the inn have money and goods, and when they will proceed on their journey:

It holds current that I told you yesternight. There's a franklin in the
wild of Kent hath brought three hundred marks with him in gold:
I heard him tell it to one of his company last night at supper. . . .
They are up already and call for eggs and butter; they will away
presently. (*1 Henry IV*, II.i.57–65)

They are thereafter robbed by Falstaff and others.

To the east of London stood a tower, part of which was used to house
dangerous offenders. In fact, part of this tower was called the Bloody
Tower (Schoenbaum 1987, pp. 123–24). Prisoners were conveyed to the
tower on boats by way of a covered channel through an entrance called
the Traitors' Gate. It is believed that at night ghosts haunted the corridors
and staircases of the tower—the same ghosts feared by Richard III before
the battle of Bosworth.

It is important to note that the 1500s were marred by poverty and its
resulting consequences: idleness, crime, prostitution, disease, and begging. G. Salgado contends that, to some extent, people who engaged in
this lower culture were somewhat organized in their criminal and deviant pursuits: they had some sort of a heirarchy (1977, p. 131). Pories
notes in her dissertation that poverty plagued England as a result of
"inflation, food shortages, and the practice of enclosure" (1995, p. 22). In
addition, the English currency was devalued in the 1500s by King Henry
VII. This fact, coupled with Somerset's military campaigns, increased
inflation. Poor harvest caused by unfavorable weather hiked the prices
of food (p. 31). The extreme poverty that permeated England at this time
was reflected in Shakespeare's Henry plays.

The practice of enclosure was instituted in England sometime around
the beginning of the fifteenth century and persisted one full century. The
practice, which restricted the amount of land landowners could give out
for pasture and tillage, was undertaken to improve agricultural soil, but
it deprived the poor of grazing rights and therefore increased their level
of poverty. Enclosure did not signify a breaking down of feudalism; it
was, rather, an ill-conceived plan to improve agriculture. By the beginning of the seventeenth century, it was clear that the practice had failed
in its intent because less than 3 percent of the country's agriculture had
been affected (Reese 1964, pp. 352–53).

The economy of England had been in a deep recession since 1570, and
this condition reached its peak in the 1580s. Corn dealers hoarded their
crop in order to get higher prices from foreign markets. Shortages of
grain at home resulted in riots as the prices rose far beyond the means
of the poor. Although legislation was drafted in 1586 to ration food to
the poor, by 1597 the subsistence conditions of the poor in England called
for great concern (Pories 1995, p. 108). In addition to the existing problems, three years of severe cold weather, and heavy rains, led to a series

of harvest failures which made grain a very scarce commodity (see Pories 1995, pp. 108–9, for detailed effects on the various counties of England).

The food shortage was not the only problem facing England; unemployment was also on the rise (1995, p. 109). An increase in the rural exodus increased the migrant population in London. Jobs were hard to get, and unskilled workers willing to accept jobs at lower pay deprived skilled workers of jobs. An increase in occupational mobility created a decline in specialized labor and specific goods and also increased unemployment levels.

This period was also marked by the plague which was responsible for approximately 14 percent of the deaths in England between 1580 and 1650. London, and various towns in England hard hit by this dwindling economy, saw a rise in the number of riots and protests. In addition to the poor, there was a steady rise in the number of rogues, drunkards, vagabonds, beggars, prostitutes, and sick people (Schoenbaum 1987, p. 126). In 1589, after an expedition against Portugal by Drake's army was unsuccessful, the discharged army returned to England to swell the ranks of the unemployed. Many of them, still fully equipped with their weapons, resorted to vagrancy or armed robbery (Salgado 1977, p. 117). Another group which increased the problem of vagrancy included former employees of monasteries. After Henry VIII dissolved the monasteries, employees such as gardeners, cooks, and others lost their jobs. Those who could not find other legitimate ways of earning a living became vagrants. In addition, after the Reformation abolished the existence of Frairs and Pardoners who wandered throughout England, many of them turned to vagrancy (1977, pp. 117–19).

The government was divided in its response to these conditions. Some members of parliament voted to ban the practice of enclosure and, instead, create an open house (free access to land) for the poor. Other members resented a ban on enclosure and showed little sympathy for the problems of the poor. The resulting legislature was full of contradictions. On the one hand, provisions were made to assist the poor; on the other hand, factions of the legislature were punitive (Pories 1995, pp. 113–23). On the local level, control was exerted over the activities of the lower class. Some groups of this class were singled out for help, while the others were excluded from relief because they were deemed responsible for their fate. A proliferation of alehouses were used as meeting places for the destitute, prostitutes, vagabonds, and rioters. By the seventeenth century, there were increasing numbers of petitions to close these alehouses (1995, p. 123).

The plight of the poor drew the attention of literary writers as well. Shakespeare, for instance, created the character of Falstaff, in the Henry plays, in part, to depict the idleness, prostitution, and life in the alehouses that prevailed in England at the time. Salgado depicts alehouses at that time as breeding grounds for deviance and crime and, more important, warehouses for stolen property (1977, p. 131). Those in dire need of food or money hung out in these alehouses, and it was not uncommon for parents to allow their daughters to become prostitutes in the alehouses. Shakespeare exposed the condition of the poor aptly when Falstaff recruited the raggedy poor as soldiers for the king. Pories contends that, in 1 Henry VI, Shakespeare is criticizing the government's practices of minimizing the problems of poverty and its effects on the people (1995, p. 139). When Prince Hal engages in the same activities for which he passes judgment on Falstaff, Shakespeare, in effect, is illustrating that the government's response to poverty was based on a simplified conception of the social conditions of the poor. The rejection of Falstaff by Prince Hal at the end illustrates the rejection of the have-nots in Shakespeare's England in favor of the haves.

Shakespeare's time was, of course, prescientific, and the writings at the time dealt mostly with people and their lives. Prior to his stay in London, Shakespeare had lived only in Stratford. Life in Stratford could be compared to a gemeinschaft-oriented society. In this kind of society, traditional folkways and close intimate human contact are preserved. Conformity to existing norms and mores is spontaneous, and the behavior of any one person is similar, if not identical, to that of the other members of the community.

London, on the other hand, experienced extensive contact with other European cities. Commercial activities flourished via sea and on land. New trades, arts, and crafts were introduced as traders interacted with one another. With the increase in transciency, and population heterogeneity, London became a society characterized by impersonal relationships, competition, and a decline in traditional norms and values. In essence, London was a gesellschaft-oriented society (see Tonnies 1887 for a full understanding of gemeinschaft and gesellschaft).

In medieval England, it was common to refer to travelers as "thieves" mainly because of their mobility and anonymity. These conditions rendered it difficult to detect criminals and to implement official social control. Writing centuries later about social change, W. F. Ogburn (1952) suggested that rapid changes in technology could create conditions whereby the criminal laws, which were written for social conditions that prevailed prior to the technological changes, would likely be violated. Although technological advancement was not as rapid in Shakespeare's England as it was when Ogburn wrote, it is not utterly wrong to suggest that his assertions might have been applicable during the Renaissance in England.

An increase in the migrant population in England at that time possibly generated some culture conflict because the dominant English culture clashed with the migrant culture. Some behavior that was legitimate in the migrant tradition suddenly became illegal in the English culture.

Similar conditions in France in the late eighteenth century may have inspired Emile Durkheim to write *The Division of Labor in Society* (1893) and *Suicide* (1897). Durkheim distinguished between a "mechanical" society and an "organic" society. A society characterized by "mechanical solidarity" is one that is governed by established rules, values, and morals. The "organic solidarity" is a society in which members depend on one another, and roles are specialized. Durkheim was of the opinion that crime was inevitable because of the heterogeneity in society. Because people have different needs, and because each person has his or her own way of meeting these needs, crime is a normal and necessary social behavior. Crime, Durkheim postulates, may often imply the need for social change.

Although Shakespeare's writings pre-date those of Tonnies and Durkheim, the analogy here, and the discussion in the following paragraphs, demonstrate some of the same dilemmas facing society at various eras. These concepts are worthy of mention because the changing structure of modern postindustrial society still has a profound bearing on "intergroup and interpersonal relationships" (see Siegel 1983, p. 165). J. A. Sharpe, for instance, indicates that a "criminal class" was deemed to exist in England because of speedy industrialization and urbanization (1984 p. 94). These processes, as he explained, generated a structural difference within the English society. The miserably poor in the society lived in distinct neighborhoods characterized by filth, uncouthness in speech, and degenerative morals. Until the advent of a radical approach to criminology, those within this class of society were automatically stereotyped as criminals (Sharpe 1984, p. 94). In addition, it was deemed that "poor toilet training, irregular church attendance, and an unwillingness (when of an appropriate age) to participate in youth club activities" led people to criminality. In essence, with economic and social change, came an insurgence of a criminal class—those who were unable to keep pace with the changing times.

Following the Renaissance, a new class of writers emerged. These writers, many of whom were classified as social philosophers, discussed human relations with the institution of government. According to S. Souryal, the social contract theory developed in response to human enlightenment and civic awareness (1992, p. 66). Souryal explains that this social paradigm is "based on the belief that natural existence without a binding agreement among those who live together can create danger for all concerned" (1992, p. 66). The early advocates of this theory were Thomas Hobbes (1588–1679), John Locke (1632–1704), and Montesquieu (1689–1755).

Hobbes, an English philosopher, was twenty-eight years old when

Shakespeare died in 1616. The ninety-one years Hobbes lived were characterized by political turmoil in England. While Shakespeare wrote about human relations in an exploratory way, Hobbes was prescriptive in his writings. Hobbes was of the opinion that if humans were left to pursue their own individual interests, there would seldom be any "cooperation and exchange" among them. Rather, they would use any deviant means necessary to fulfill their self-interests (see Edgerton 1976, p. 4). Therefore, to control deviant behavior, Hobbes suggested that unfettered rights be accorded the state to use force to maintain social order. Hobbes was sympathetic toward the king and espoused his views declaring the king an absolute monarch, and asserted that a social contract with his subjects was necessary. In his social contract, Hobbes stated that "everyone gives up his right of governing himself and authorizes a designated person or assembly of men to govern his actions on the condition that every other citizen does the same and abides with the authority of the said person or assembly" (quoted in Souryal 1992, p. 67). It is only through this method that social civility could be obtained.

In his plays that relate to rulers and matters of state (for example, the *Henry* plays, *Julius Caesar*, and *Richard II*), and those that deal with the relationships between people within society and the public actions that govern them (for example, *Measure for Measure* and *Love's Labour's Lost*), Shakespeare, without declaring how government and its people should coexist, simply interpreted group psychology while observing political behavior (Morris 1953, p. 103).

Locke provided a different dimension to Hobbes' ideas. Although he agreed with Hobbes, he advocated a more liberal form of government because he had more respect for peoples' moral judgment. To him, an absolute monarchy was inconsistent with civil society (Thilly 1914). Locke believed that people were basically "pleasant chaps" and therefore did not deserve rigorous government interference in their lives (Souryal 1992, p. 67). He believed that social order could be achieved if a "natural identity of interests" could be upheld and shared (Edgerton 1976, p. 4).

In France, Montesquieu, in *Esprit des lois* (1748), advocated a government that provided "adequate standards of justice, happiness, and morality" (Souryal 1992, p. 68). According to Souryal, Montesquieu located the origin of ethics in the presence of laws which are to be obeyed because they are good in themselves. Montesquieu's book has generally been regarded as the charter of society and the beginning of modern-day legal systems.

LAW DURING SHAKESPEARE'S TIME

The Elizabethan legal system comprised three common law courts: the court of Queens/Kings Bench, the Court of Common Pleas, and the

Court of Exchequer. There was a dualism of the English legal system. Chancery courts, or Equity courts, were separate from the three common law courts until the Judicature Act of 1873. Chancery courts dealt with issues that were outside the scope of common law courts. Because only the chancery courts practiced mitigated justice, parties who needed a fair trial took their cases to the chancery courts. During this period, the principle of equity was gradually gaining ground. In 1330 King Edward III had accorded the chancellor (a chief judge of the court of chancery) the right to hear cases that other judges would not hear. The court of the Lord Chancellor was the Court of Equity. The two types of courts—the common law courts and the equity courts—engaged in two different systems of jurisprudence. The common law courts instituted action *in rem*, that is, against the thing or property of the claimants without making reference to their individual titles (for example, land), while the equity courts acted *in personam*. Actions *in personam* sought judgment against persons involving their personal rights based on the jurisdiction of their person. These two courts remained separate until the Judicature Act of 1873.

Although the two courts had separate jurisdictions, it became evident that the Court of Equity was increasingly encroaching on the jurisdiction of the common law courts. By 1596 or 1597, it was obvious that the two courts were engaged in a power struggle. At this time, Shakespeare was already a playwright in London, Sir Edward Coke had become judge of the Court of Common Pleas, Lord Ellesmere (formerly Thomas Egerton) had become Lord Chancellor, and Francis Bacon was a prominent lawyer of Gray's Inn. About this time, when the legal quibble between the two courts intensified, Shakespeare wrote *The Merchant of Venice*, which dramatizes the conflict between the common law and equity. Equity prevailed.

The decision in *Glanvill v. Courtney* (1615), an actual case that was brought to the Court of Common Law for trial, seems to have been inspired by the decision made in the trial scene in *The Merchant of Venice* (Andrews 1969, p. xii). *Glanvill v. Courtney*, as in *The Merchant of Venice*, concerned the execution of the terms of a bond. Although the Court of Common Law entered judgment for the plaintiff, the Court of Equity issued an injunction precluding the plaintiff from carrying out the terms of the bond. King James I, upon the advice of a commission led by Sir Francis Bacon, decided in favor of equity. Thereafter, he who did equity, received equity.

The common law courts and equity courts were not the only courts in existence at the time. There were courts of specific jurisdiction—the Court of Augmentations, the Church Court, the Court of Star Chamber, among others. Initially, the Court of Star Chamber sat with no jury and could dispense any punishment other than the death penalty. However, it gradually extended its jurisdiction until it simply became too dreadful for the English. It was eventually abolished.

The common law was especially appreciated by the educated class in England because it was perceived as not being as coercive and as arbitrary as the laws in such countries as France. The rich also placed a lot of faith in the common law because it protected their property rights. The popular impression at the time was that humans were innately evil; therefore, "good laws" were needed to prevent anarchy. A good portion of the population was versed in the laws of the land and others acquired knowledge of the law after they infringed upon it or when they became litigants (Sharpe 1984, pp. 144–45; Keeton 1967, p. 3). It is contended that Shakespeare's knowledge of the law derived from his roles as "litigant, witness, or even as a person who entered into a variety of legal transactions" (Keeton 1967, p. 3).

Although many educated people perceived the law as fair, there were others who viewed it as oppressive. The legal profession was highly popular at the time, although there were segments of society (for example, literary writers) who held lawyers in low esteem (Sharpe 1984, p. 146).

Religion played a pivotal role in shaping people's perception of the law. Much of the population believed that the law and law enforcers were necessary to curb the iniquity that shrouded humans. Sharpe cites the opinion of some with regard to this issue: " 'Magistrates in towns and corporations carry and draw the sword for the maintenance of peace and civill order: it is well done for it is a worke of their calling' "; a magistrate " 'beares the sword specially for the good of men's souls . . . magistracy and government be necessary in the societies of Christian' " (William Perkins, quoted in 1984, p. 151).

Religion also played a role in shaping Shakespeare's ideas about the moral and legal fallibility of man. Although laws are enacted in order to minimize social conflict, Shakespeare's religious orientation led him to believe that, because we are all sinners, even those charged with the responsibility of enforcing the law can sometimes transgress it. This is what W. G. Knight alludes to as Shakespeare's "earthly, humanly warm, approach to the spiritualistic truth" (1967, p. 11). In *Hamlet*, Claudius commits murder. Bothered by his conscience, he resorts to prayer and repentance, as demanded of sinners by Christian doctrine. In *Measure for Measure*, Angelo, in his position as interim duke, condemns Claudio for a sexual sin—a sin he himself later commits. While dying, he tries to resort to prayer. In *The Merchant of Venice*, Portia tries unsuccessfully to evoke from Shylock "mercy," a virtue which "blesseth him that gives and him that takes" (1967, pp. 228–30). P. Milward also draws a parallel between Shakespeare's *Othello* and the Biblical story of the Garden of Eden and the fall of man (1987, p. 61). According to Milward, *Othello* can be likened to Adam, Desdemona to Eve, and Iago to the serpent, Satan. Milward points out that a slight twist in the story exists: Othello is tempted, not Desdemona; and the temptation was against Desdemona.

The most common types of punishment were whipping for petty offenses, such as begging, and incarceration, for petty theft. The death penalty was implemented for aggravated theft, robbery, murder, and sometimes even for relatively minor offenses, such as fornication and theft. Salgado notes that the death penalty was a foregone conclusion for anyone arrested for highway robbery (1977, p. 121). Anyone found guilty of a felony was sentenced to death. In effect, therefore, as Keeton stated, "The law frustrated its main object—the suppression of crime—by its undiscriminating brutality" (1967, p. 38).

"Shaming" as a type of punishment was also used during that period although, by the 1700s, there was a move away from it. Shaming was intended to achieve two things: to make the offender and offense known to the whole community and to humiliate the offender publicly so that he or she would desist from criminal activities in the future. Sharpe cites several examples of shaming. A woman found guilty of embezzling wool worth 4d was put in the stocks at Shepton Mallet with a lock of wool hung on her on a market day. Everyone who went to the market on that day saw her (1984, p. 178).

Although punishment was an obvious and necessary means of maintaining peace and order, the rich and powerful could contravene the law in order to fortify or legitimize their position. In a sense, this meant that the crimes of the powerful could be overlooked by the law because these people were deemed socially useful.

Shakespeare mirrored society in this light in some of his plays. D. Cohen (1993) studied the legitimization of violence in 1 Henry IV. The purpose of Cohen's study was to look at violence that was made lawful because it was carried out by "the court of the rich and powerful." Cohen argued that the violence in 1 Henry IV was intended to "glorify physical violence as a necessary force of morality" (1993, p. 30). Hal's killing of Hotspur was a "socially useful idea of the possibility of violence being good—moral, legitimate, and, even sacred" (pp. 30–31). Cohen's analysis suggests that, because of the "sacred historical tradition," the violence in 1 Henry IV was necessary. Therefore, the motive for the murder of Hotspur was "legalized and made to supply a social need" (p. 31): to end violence and restore authority.

Informal social control gained some ground in England at that time because both the common law and the ecclesiastical law endorsed it. Whenever parties to a suit expressed willingness to settle their dispute privately, the authorities usually granted their wishes. In the 1580s, for instance, authorities in the town of Warwick entertained a plaintiff's requests to withdraw theft charges on defendants if the latter were willing to settle the issue out of court (Sharpe 1984, p. 179). It appears, however, that, sometime in the 1700s, the practice of informal social control gave way to formal court trials because of new policies that required harsher sanctions on criminals.

The philosophical bases for punishment at the time were deterrence and rehabilitation. With no clear-cut methods of determining whether a particular punishment was proportionate to the crime or, indeed, whether the punishment fitted the crime, local authorities sometimes devised irrational punishments as appropriate methods of redressing the wrong. Sharpe cites the example of some reputed Somerset parents of a bastard who, in 1617, were whipped until their bodies became bloody, "with two fiddles being played before them 'in regard to make known their lewdness in begetting the said base child upon sabbath day coming from dancyng'" (1984, p. 178).

Increasingly during that period, the therapeutic idea began to gain ground although its implementation differed from contemporary therapeutic notions. "A healthy dose of labour discipline" was deemed to be a panacea for criminality. Prisons (houses of correction) found the idea of hard labor very promising:

> [The] main aim was to make the labour power of unwilling people socially useful. By being forced to work within the institution, the prisoners would form industrious habits and would receive a vocational training at the same time. When released, it was hoped they would voluntarily swell the labour market. (G. Rusche and O. Kirchheimer 1939, quoted in Sharpe 1984, p. 179)

Skepticism existed then as now as to the effectiveness of correctional facilities. Houses of correction were more holding places for deviants and petty offenders than places for reformation. Vagrants, renegades, beggars, and other deviants and petty offenders were sent to those houses. In the 1610s it was not uncommon to find people who had been acquitted of theft to be locked up in houses of corrections merely because society still perceived them to be somewhat degenerate (1984, p. 180). Although these houses were used to punish, their efficacy in curbing recidivism was much in question. In 1621 a draft bill, reflecting the skepticism about the productivity of houses of correction, was presented to parliament.

> Long imprisonment in common gaoles rendreth such offenders the more obdurate and desperate when they are delivered out of the gaols, they being then poor, miserable, and friendless, are in a manner exposed to the like mischiefs, they not having means of ther owne, nor place of habitation nor likely to gaigne so much credite

from any honest householder as to interteyn them. (Commons Debates, 1612, quoted in Sharpe 1984, p. 182)

It is obvious that the supposed benefits of correctional facilities have been a constant issue since the Middle Ages.

SUMMARY

To be properly understood, Shakespeare's plays should be read within their historical context. This chapter reviews the lives of those who lived in Shakespearean times and the plight they encountered as a result of the forces of nature, politics, religious persecutions, and, in some measure, their own actions. The chapter also summarizes legal responses to crime at that time. The responses ranged from approving of out-of-court settlements, to utilizing draconian measures in an effort to ameliorate soaring levels of criminal activities. It seems evident that Shakespeare's writings were not based on imaginary themes; rather, they reflected social activities and problems of the time.

One of the biggest social issues was unemployment. With the population growing more rapidly than industrialization, a vast number of people found it difficult to find jobs. The consequence was a soaring number of vagrants, thieves, beggars, prostitutes, sick people, and a host of other deviants and criminals. The response of the rulers was inadequate, and the judicial system handed down severe penalties even for offenses that were minor. Not everyone suffered from the dwindling economy. Rich merchants, lawyers, entertainers, and bankers, among others, prospered while others suffered.

The common law courts engaged in a different jurisprudence of law from equity courts. While the common law courts handled actions *in rem*, the equity courts acted *in personam*. Although it was apparent that there was friction between the two courts, they remained separate until the Judicature Act of 1873.

PART II

CRIMES AND DEVIANCE COMMITTED BY SELECTED CHARACTERS

INTRODUCTION

Shakespeare introduced in his plays a wide variety of criminal and deviant characters. Some of the crimes committed in the plays represent illegal behavior acknowledged universally as *mala in se*; that is, "wrong in themselves." These crimes include murder, robbery, rape, and theft. Some characters commit offenses that are *mala prohibita*—acts that are made offenses by statute—which could carry criminal sanctions in some situations. The weight given to *mala prohibita* crimes differs from society to society, and also from time to time. Many of the offenses characterized as *mala in se* would also be considered deviant—morally wrong though perhaps not illegal.

Crimes may also be classified according to their seriousness and type of punishment. Felonies, for instance, are serious or grave offenses, such as murder. The punishment for a felony may range from imprisonment in a state or federal penitentiary to execution. Misdemeanors are less serious offenses, such as petty theft, and the punishments range from a fine or probation to time in jail, not exceeding one year. Infractions or violations are the least serious offenses. They may be infringements against traffic laws. The punishment is usually a fine.

Crimes can also be classified based on the subject matter.

Rape, for instance, is a crime against the person; the burning of a dwelling is a crime against habitation. Some crimes may fall under two categories. Robbery, for instance, may be a crime against the person and also a crime against property.

In Shakespeare's time, fornication was a crime punishable by the death penalty. It is worthy of mention that treason in Shakespeare's England was a crime against the sovereign; the killing of a sovereign was treason. This point is relevant because the definition of treason in the U.S. Constitution does not expressly include the killing of a president. Anyone who killed the president would probably be charged with assassination, not treason. The killing of Duncan is discussed under murder/treason because that was treason in English law. In addition, although Richard III's crimes are politically motivated, some of his killings cannot be classified as treason, for instance, the killings of Clarence and Hastings (people with no political position). The killings he engages in in order to solidify his position after he becomes king are repressive and thereby place his acts under state crimes.

Part II is subdivided into three chapters: Chapter 3 describes violence against the person; Chapter 4 considers property crimes; and Chapter 5 concerns lesser wrongs, noncriminal types of deviant behavior.

Table 1 summarizes Shakespeare's characters and the type of crime or deviance associated with the play in the sample.

Table 1
Fictional Offenders in a Sampling of Selected Plays

Criminal/Deviant Act	Theatrical Character	Play
Violence against the Person		
Murder	Richard III	*Richard III*
Murder	Othello	*Othello*
Murder/treason	Macbeth	*Macbeth*
Accessory before and after the fact	Lady Macbeth	*Macbeth*
Attempt at committing "grievous bodily harm"	Shylock	*The Merchant of Venice*
Attempted murder	Iago	*Othello*
Criminal solicitation	Iago	*Othello*

Criminal/Deviant Act	Theatrical Character	Play
Property Crimes		
Robbery	Falstaff	*1 Henry IV*
Embezzlement/misappropriation	Falstaff	*1 Henry IV*
Theft	Pompey	*Measure for Measure*
Noncriminal Deviance		
Suicide	Lady Macbeth	*Macbeth*
Alcoholism	Falstaff	*1 Henry IV*
Vagrancy	Froth	*Measure for Measure*
Nonviolent Sexual Deviance		
Fornication/social corruption	Angelo	*Measure for Measure*
Fornication	Claudio	*Measure for Measure*

3

Violence against the Person

Murder "is the unlawful killing of a human being by another with malice aforethought, express or implied" (Black 1990, p. 1019). The words "malice aforethought" in the common law definition have been conceptualized differently over time. Those jurisdictions in the United States that have chosen to use neither the common law definition nor the *Model Penal Code* definition tend to define murder based on the intent of the murderer. They categorize killings according to degree. The *Model Penal Code* (section 210.2) defines murder as a first degree felony when (1) it is committed purposely or knowingly or (2) it is committed recklessly under circumstances manifesting extreme indifference to the value of human life. Such recklessness and indifference are presumed if the actor is engaged, or is an accomplice, committing or attempting to commit, or is fleeing after committing or attempting to commit a robbery, rape or deviate sexual intercourse by force or threat of force, arson, burglary, kidnapping, or felonious escape.

Common law distinguishes three kinds of homicide:

Justifiable homicide: This occurs when a person acts in self-defense or in the line of duty, including homicides committed by police officers while on the job and state-sanctioned executions.

Excusable homicide: This occurs when a person is incapable of understanding what he or she is doing, for example, while insane. It may also include an accidental homicide.

Criminal homicide: this includes reckless and negligent homicides and those committed knowingly or purposefully.

The law distinguishes between different kinds of killings based on the killer's mental state.

First-degree murder: This homicide is premeditated and committed with deliberation. Some states refer to first-degree murder as capital murder. Courts have concluded that the premeditation need not be done over a period of time; one can premeditate at the spur of the moment. Some states include, in this category, the killing of a law enforcement officer, any killings that occur during the commission of a felony, and the killing of an infant. Also included in this category are atrocious murders—those that entail extreme savagery or cruelty.

Second-degree murder: Killings that occur without premeditation are categorized as second-degree murder. They may occur during the commission of another crime, or while acting recklessly or with a "depraved heart." The intent may not have been to kill but to cause grave bodily harm.

Voluntary manslaughter: These killings are triggered by provocation but are void of premeditation.

Involuntary manslaughter: These killings occur recklessly but without deliberation.

MURDER: RICHARD III

The type of killing pertinent to this discussion is first-degree murder—murders that are deliberate and leave no doubt in the mind that the intent was to take away the life of the victim. Although Richard himself was handicapped and thus could not do the actual killings, he hired murderers to do the killings for him. He used his position to exercise terror. His actions were premeditated and carefully designed.

Richard III commits a series of calculated killings. All his criminal pursuits are well planned—"plans have I laid, inductions dangerous" (I.i.36)—and carried out with a wanton disregard for those whom he slaughters. Richard begins his criminal pursuits by vowing to "prove a villain" and to set his "brother Clarence and the king in deadly hate the one against the other . . . with lies well steel'd with weighty arguments" (I.i.38–39, 156). The anticipated result is that Clarence will be killed, frail King Edward V will die, and the crown will be Richard's.

Richard sets out to accomplish his goals by hiring murderers to kill Clarence. He instructs them to "be sudden in the execution" (I.iii.355), to be obdurate, and not to listen to Clarence's plea for mercy. The murderers approach Clarence while he is asleep. When he is awakened by their debating whether he should be killed while he sleeps, the murderers apprise him of their intent. He tries to dissuade them from the act, but the murderers stab and kill him nevertheless.

Richard employs another kind of weapon: his wit. He uses his wit to feign honesty even to those who know all too well his evil intentions. He pretentiously laments over Clarence's death and falsely blames the death on the queen and her allies. With his wit, he is usually able to persuade someone to do something dishonest.

He goes about his evil designs by professing to be a man of God: "I clothe my naked villainy with odd old ends stol'n forth of holy writ; and seem a saint when most I play a devil" (I.iii.344–46). By means of cunning devices and false promises, he makes almost everyone accept his disloyalty and dishonesty, and he skillfully suborns his associates to commit murder. When Buckingham, one of his allies, asks Richard what they will do if their other ally, Hastings, does not approve of their plots to arrogate the royal seat, Richard, without any qualms responds, "[C]hop off his head . . . and when I am king, claim thou of me the earldom of Hereford" (III.i.193–95).

Hastings refuses to be part of the conspiracy, and, although Richard appears cheerful in the council meeting, he harbors malicious thoughts about Hastings and looks for an excuse to get rid of him. Richard uses Hastings' expression of his doubts about Richard's assertion that Queen Elizabeth used witchcraft to wither his arm as a pretext to behead Hastings. With carefully crafted lies, Richard convinces the mayor that Hastings is a traitor (guilty of treason) to which the mayor responds, "Now, fair befall you! he deserv'd his death; And you my good lords, both, have well proceeded to warn false traitors from the like attempts" (III.v.54–56).

Richard is appointed king by the council, a post he pretends to be reluctant to accept. He knows Prince Edward's heirs are alive and have stronger claims to the throne. He therefore wishes "the bastards dead; and I would have it suddenly perform'd" in order to "stop all hopes whose growth may damage me [Richard]" (IV.ii.27–28, 77). Buckingham, his closest ally, is hesitant to participate in the murder of Edward's sons. Richard, now king, is infuriated and hires a murderer who massacres the children in their sleep. Richard thereafter breaks his promise to reward Buckingham with the dukedom of Hereford. Fearing for his life, Buckingham deserts Richard.

M. Rousseau discusses Richard's crimes. He describes Richard as a tyrant who replaces the law with violence. Richard's worst crime, Rousseau states, is his abuse of the people under the pretext that violence is legitimate (1981, pp. 40–43).

Richard is a criminal who combines impudence with a knack for persuasion to exploit his victims' weaknesses. He talks Lady Anne into marrying him in the presence of her husband's corpse, whom Richard had killed. He marries Anne, knowing that he will have her "but will not keep her long" (I.ii.246). This indeed he does.

MURDER: OTHELLO

The killing of Desdemona is also a first-degree murder. When a killing is premeditated and done deliberately it is first-degree murder. Othello premeditated his action over a long period of time during which he looked for justification for his intended crime and the most suitable method to employ in the killing. Legally, and in fact, Othello had no justification for the murder other than his own gullibility. Furthermore, he tormented his victim before he finally killed her, aggravating his crime.

Othello's love for Desdemona became clouded when Iago systematically filled Othello's mind with false tales of her infidelity. Othello laments as he plans revenge:

She's gone. I am abus'd; and my relief must be to loathe her. O curse of marriage, that we can call these delicate creatures ours, and not their appetites! I had rather be a toad . . . than keep a corner in the thing I love for others' uses. (III.iii.332–38).

As the false evidence of Desdemona's infidelity mounts, Othello's sentiments change from love to loathing and eventually to destruction. "All my fond love" is gone, he confesses, and "my bloody thoughts, with violent pace, shall never look back . . . till that a capable and wide revenge swallow them up" (III.iii.545, 560–63).

The murder is cruel. Desdemona is tormented emotionally before she is killed, and she is never given an opportunity to explain her innocence. The epithets Othello piles on her—"whore," "public commoner," "impudent strumpet"—are degrading enough to cause a colossal depression. Although Othello is determined to "chop her into messes" (IV.i.240) Desdemona is "smothered" in bed as she begs Othello to let her say a final prayer.

MURDER/TREASON: MACBETH

The most serious crime a citizen can commit against his or her country or government is treason, and the most serious crime a person can commit against another person is murder. In early England, treason was defined as the "killing of the king, queen, or the king's eldest son; violating the queen; counterfeiting the king's money; or slaying judges on duty" (Sigler 1981, p. 167). Modern statutes do not define treason in the same way although a common theme runs through all statutes that relate to treason: breach of loyalty to one's government. The U.S. Constitution, Article III, Section 3, defines treason in the following manner:

> Treason against the United States, shall consist only in levying War against them, or in adhering to their enemies, giving them Aid and Comfort. No person shall be convicted of Treason unless on the Testimony of two Witnesses to the same overt Act, or on Confession in open court.

According to H. Black (1990, p. 1501), treason relates to "a breach of allegiance to one's government, usually committed through levying war against such government or by giving aid or comfort to the enemy." The elements of the crime therefore include:

1. Allegiance to one's government. In this regard, government may mean state or federal government. State treason laws are not applied in cases of treason against the United States because that falls within the domain of the federal government.
2. A criminal intent manifested by any act that breaches the accused's loyalty to the government.

In order to be prosecuted for treason, the offender must be a citizen of the United States. Although criminal law requires noncitizens conform to U.S. laws, they do not owe allegiance to this country. Any crimes they perpetrate against the United States cannot be referred to as treason. Some other classification will be used.

In English law, high treason is a crime against the sovereign. When one kills a sovereign, it is not only an assassination but also a breach of loyalty to one's country. Therefore, when Macbeth killed the king he not only committed murder, he committed treason.

When he commits his first criminal act, Macbeth appears to lack the sangfroid of a typical criminal—a criminal whose conscience does not bother him. He wavers in his intention to kill Duncan, the king, as he considers what good the king had accomplished and the effects the crime would have on his own reputation: "He hath honour'd me of late. . . . I have bought golden opinions from all sorts of people, which would be worn now in their newest gloss, not cast aside so soon" (I.vii.33–35).

Macbeth nonetheless carries out the assassination. He and his wife carefully plan Duncan's murder at a time when the king is most vulnerable—when he is their house guest, while he is sound asleep, and while his guards sleep drugged by alcohol. Lady Macbeth treacherously lays down the scheme:

> When Duncan is asleep,—whereto the rather shall his day's hard journey soundly invite him, his two chamberlains will I with wine and wassail so convince that memory, the warder of the brain, shall be a fume, and the receipt of reason a limbec only: when in swinish sleep their drenched natures lie as in death, what cannot you and I perform upon the unguarded Duncan? (I.vii.66–75)

Suffering from a weakness of resolve to say no to Lady Macbeth's devilish intent, Macbeth moves stealthily "like a Ghost" with "ravishing strides" (II.i.59–60) toward his victim and, with a dagger, stabs Duncan to death while he sleeps.

After the crime is accomplished, Macbeth is unable to be at peace with himself. He is puzzled at the sight of his bloody hands, wonders if they are his, and expresses horror at what the hands had done.

After one murder Macbeth becomes desensitized and, almost as though he never resented being pushed into committing his crime, brazenly sets out, with the help of hired assassins, to massacre subjects loyal to the late king. First he plots Banquo's murder. The crime has to be carried out in the night, and no trace of evidence can be left behind: "I require a clearness: and with him . . . to leave no rubs nor botches in the work" (III.i.138–39). In addition, he instructs the murderers to get rid of Fleance, Banquo's son: Fleance "must embrace the fate of the dark hour" (III.i.142–43). Macbeth becomes reaffirmed in his resolve to destroy anyone who might challenge his right to the throne. When Macduff, a potential challenger to the throne, escapes his wrath, he is determined to slaughter the rest of the Macduffs.

> . . . from this moment the very fistlings of my heart
> Shall be the fistlings of my hand. And even now,
> To crown my thoughts with acts, be it thought and done:
> The castle of Macduff I will surprise;
> Seize upon Fife; give to the edge o' the sword
> His wife, his babes, and all unfortunate souls
> That trace him in his line. (IV.i.150–57)

Macbeth finally becomes completely detached from any remorse and earns the epithets "bloodier villain," "tyrant," and "butcher."

ACCESSORY BEFORE AND AFTER THE FACT: LADY MACBETH

The doctrine of complicity has long been recognized by both common law and Anglo-American law. Accomplices, or parties to a crime, were distinguished at common law based on their involvement in the crime in order to determine the appropriate punishment for each participant. For felonies, the distinction was not necessary as each participant was treated as a felon. The need for categorization of participation became all the more obvious when the English society began to experience a decline in crime rates. Four parties to a crime were distinguished:

Principals in the first degree: These are the ones who actually commit the crime. In a crime of murder, for instance, these are the ones who pull the trigger or thrust the dagger into the victim.

Principals in the second degree: These people provide assistance at the time the crime is committed. Their presence at the crime scene is relevant: They notify the actual perpetrator of the arrival of someone not connected to the crime; they prevent the victim from escaping; they drive a getaway vehicle; or they perform other acts that facilitate the commission of the crime.

Accessories before the fact: They usually are not present at the crime scene, but they abet and assist in the crime in other ways. They may, for instance, provide the know-how, divulge secret knowledge about how best to carry out the plot, or provide weapons and ammunition necessary for the crime. They may even lure the victim to the crime scene.

Accessories after the fact: These people provide aid and solace to the principal in the first degree. They may provide travel documents and money to the perpetrator to enable the latter escape. They may conceal evidence or provide false information in order to mislead police officers. They may also provide a haven, or disguises, to the perpetrator to stall efforts to find him or her.

Most contemporary statutes avoid the distinction and treat accessories before the fact and participants during the crime as principals. Those who otherwise would be accessories to a crime can be prosecuted and convicted even if the primary offender is never brought to justice. The courts determine that a person is an accomplice to a crime when there is evidence of a specific intent to provide assistance in the commission of a crime.

According to this discussion, Lady Macbeth's role as an accomplice is evident. As an accessory before the fact, she psychologically instilled a criminal mind-set in Macbeth, and she was responsible for getting the king's guards drunk to facilitate Macbeth's access to the king. As an accessory after the fact, she not only instructed Macbeth on how to cover up the crime, she assisted him in concealing the evidence. In addition, she engaged in framing the king's guards as the murderers.

Lady Macbeth is an altruistic criminal who is masterful and stalwart in her determination to execute Duncan. She is altruistic in the sense that she destroys out of love for her husband and her husband's benefit, not from what she stands to gain. She therefore gives no thought to the wrongness of the act nor to the consequences.

The witches' predictions about her husband's rise to power excite her, and she immediately develops a plan to kill Duncan.

> Come you spirits that tend on mortal thoughts, unsex me here; And fill me, from the crown to the toe, top-full of direst cruelty! Make thick my blood, stop up the access and passage to remorse, That no compunctious visitings of nature shake my fell purposes, nor keep peace between the effect of it! (I.v.44–51)

Thereafter, Lady Macbeth not only engaged in the arduous task of plotting the death of Duncan, but also of impressing on her husband the witches' prophecy of his greatness and instilling in him the mind-set of a murderer. She tells him to "Look like the time; bear welcome in your eye . . . look like the innocent flower, but be the serpent under't" (I.v.72–75).

Macbeth contemplates the crime, recognizes that "bloody instructions, which being taught, return to plague the inventor" (I.vii.10), and recoils from the murder plan. He tells Lady Macbeth that "we will proceed no longer in this business" (I.vii.33). Lady Macbeth, terribly infuriated, questions Macbeth: "Art thou afeard to be the same in thine own act and valour as thou art in desire?" (I.vii.34–43). She skillfully suggests that Macbeth is effeminate but if he commits the assassination "then [he] were a man" (I.vii.52).

Lady Macbeth realizes that her husband lacks the nerve to murder; therefore, she must convince him to attain what she thinks ought to be his—the crown. When Macbeth, fearful of a fiasco, asks his wife what "if we should fail?," Lady Macbeth firmly responds, "we fail! . . . and we'll not fail" (I.vii.65–66). She lays out the murder plot and a cover-up: "[W]e shall make our griefs and clamour roar upon his death" (I.vii.88–90). Macbeth, his manhood having been challenged, succumbs to his wife's taunt: "I am settled, and bend up each corporal agent to this terrible feat" (I.vii.91–92).

Lady Macbeth, fearing her husband is cowardly, embarks on her treachery alone. She gets Duncan's guards drunk, then takes a little ale herself to make her bold. She proclaims, "[W]hat hath quenched them hath given me fire" (II.i.71). She then proceeds to the place where Duncan is sleeping but does not commit the murder because, as she declares, "had he not resembled [her] father as he slept, [she] had done't" (II.i.86–87).

The act nevertheless gets done. Macbeth assassinates the king. When he expresses horror at the sight of the hands that had committed murder, Lady Macbeth chides him, "[A] foolish thought to say a sorry sight!" (II.i.101). She then explains to him how the crime can be covered up: "[G]o get some water, and wash this filthy witness from your hand" (II.i.136–37). Further, she orders him to take back the murder weapon and "smear the sleepy grooms with blood" (II.i.140–41). When Macbeth is terrified to take the weapon back to the room in which Duncan's corpse lies, Lady Macbeth is enraged and utters insulting remarks:

> infirm of purpose! give me the daggers: the sleeping and the dead are but as pictures: 'tis the eye of childhood that fears a painted devil. If he do bleed, I'll gild the faces of the grooms withal, for it must seem their guilt. (II.i.152–57)

Lady Macbeth attempts not just a cover-up; she wants Duncan's guards to be held responsible for the murder she has orchestrated and her husband has committed.

ATTEMPT AT COMMITTING "GRIEVOUS BODILY HARM": SHYLOCK

An attempted crime, or inchoate crime, is also punishable in criminal law. Although some argue that one should not be punished if one did not commit the crime, others argue that it is appropriate to punish those who fall short of completing the crime as a way of sending out a message that criminal behavior will not be tolerated. Those who argue against punishing incomplete crimes worry that, since peoples' thoughts cannot be known, unless there is an unequivocal manifestation of those thoughts through action, people should not be punished merely because they are deemed to harbor criminal thoughts. Both viewpoints have been held through the centuries.

In the sixteenth century, the English courts began to formulate guidelines to determine when a person's intent could be punished. By the start of the seventeenth century, the English courts had decided that acts that suggest preparation to commit a crime should be punished. The law with regard to attempt was clearly defined by the nineteenth century. Other inchoate crimes are conspiracy and solicitation.

Components or elements of the crime of attempt are:

1. The intent to commit a crime
2. Some manifestation (an act) of the intent
3. Failure to realize or consummate the crime.

The crime of attempt is a specific intent crime; the accused's mind-set was to commit a specific crime. The crime of attempt is distinguished from mere preparation; some states do not punish people for merely preparing to commit a crime. Four tests are used by courts to differentiate mere preparation from attempt:

Probable Desistance Approach: The courts determine whether, but for some event that frustrates an act, the crime would have been committed. That event could be the unexpected appearance of someone, bad weather, or anything else (extraneous factor) that makes the commission of the crime impossible.

Physical Proximity Doctrine: This determines how close a person came to succeeding in committing a crime.

Equivocality Approach: The courts determine that when an act exceeds the stage of being questionable, or no longer raises doubts as to the intent of the perpetrator, it no longer is mere preparation. It is an attempt (see Samaha 1996, pp. 166–67).

The Model Penal Code Standard: When the assailant has taken "substantial steps" toward carrying out the crime, it becomes an attempt.

The *Model Penal Code* standard is employed in discussing Shylock's crime. Section 5.01 of the *Model Penal Code* states:

A person is guilty of an attempt to commit a crime if, acting with the kind of culpability otherwise required for commission of the crime, he: (a) purposely engages in conduct which would constitute the crime if the attendant circumstances were as he believes them to be; or (b) when causing a particular result is an element of the crime, does or omits to do anything with the purpose of causing or with the belief that it will cause such result without further conduct on his part; or (c) purposely does or omits to do anything which, under the circumstances as he believes them to be, is an act or omission constituting a substantial step in a course of conduct planned to culminate in his commission of the crime.

Shylock's actions are discussed in the light of this definition. The law of Venice in Shakespeare's time stipulated that anyone who attempted to take away the life of a citizen, either directly or indirectly, had to forfeit his or her life and property:

It is enacted in the laws of Venice,—if it be proved against an alien, that by direct or indirect attempts he seek the life of any citizen, the party 'gainst the which he doth contrive shall seize one half his goods; the other half comes to the privy coffer of the state; and the offender's life lies in the mercy of the Duke only, 'gainst all other voice. (IV.i.348–56)

England had a similar law.

Shylock's suit against Antonio originally was a civil suit to recover a debt. Antonio borrowed from Shylock 3,000 ducats to be refunded at a certain date. The terms of the bond between Shylock and Antonio includes the cutting out of a pound of flesh from "nearest [Antonio's] heart" (IV.i.248) should Antonio fail to refund the money on the due date. Shylock's suit against Antonio to enforce the bond is in itself not criminal. His action became criminal when his attempts to enforce the bond became a specific intent to perform an act that would, if committed, be a crime. Hence, Shylock's attempt to commit grievous bodily harm to Antonio, which probably would have resulted in Antonio's death, is the crime.

Shylock is guilty of an attempt to commit a crime following the provision of the penal code. The first ingredient of attempt is that a person "purposefully engages in conduct which would constitute the crime" (*Model Penal Code*, sec. 5.01[a]). It is indicated in *The Merchant of Venice* that Shylock has a "knife whetted" (IV.i.122) and has scales ready to measure the pound of flesh. Shylock meets the first requirement as soon as he has the requisite weapon ready together with a scale to weigh Antonio's flesh. The second element of an attempt is that a person "does or omits to do anything with the belief that it will cause such result without further conduct on his part" (*Model Penal Code*, sec. 5.01[b]). When Portia requests that Shylock retain a surgeon to stop Antonio from bleeding to death, Shylock replies that the terms of the bond do not require that. Portia requests, "Have by some surgeon, Shylock, on your charge, to stop his wounds lest he do bleed to death." Shylock replies, "Is it so nominated in the bond?" (IV.i.252–55). By refusing to retain a surgeon, Shylock demonstrates that he does not care about the end result of his action.

The third ingredient of the definition of attempt is that a person "purposely does or omits to do anything which . . . constitutes a substantial step in a course of conduct planned to culminate in his commission of the crime" (*Model Penal Code*, sec. 5.01[c]). Shylock is just about to carve out the pound of flesh when Portia stops him. Shylock goes beyond mere preparation to commit a crime. His conduct is a direct step toward the commission of the act, and it is a "substantial step" in bringing about the intended result. He fails to consummate the crime only because Portia stops him. This is a criminal intent—an attempt to commit a felony.

MURDER AND ATTEMPTED MURDER: IAGO

In criminal law, an "attempt" is "an intent to commit a crime coupled with an act taken toward committing the offense" (Black 1990, p. 127). The intent needed for a crime of attempt is a specific intent. Since one's thoughts or mind-set cannot be discerned, the courts require some overt act as a manifestation of the accused's criminal purpose. Statutes draw a distinction between acts of mere preparation and criminal attempt. To constitute criminal attempt, the *Model Penal Code* stipulates that the accused must take a substantial step toward committing the crime. Section 5.01, subsection (1) (c), lists a number of acts that constitute substantial steps. Two are pertinent to the discussion of Iago's crime: (a) lying in wait, searching for or following the contemplated victim of the crime; and (b) enticing or seeking to entice the contemplated victim of the crime to go to the place contemplated for its commission.

A person may commit a crime of attempt in any one of three ways:

1. If there is a specific intent to commit a crime and that intent is established by acts that constitute a substantial step
2. When the accused purposefully engages in actions that he or she knows are criminal
3. When the accused deliberately engages in activities that help another person consummate a criminal venture, or attempt to carry out that venture.

Iago commits a crime of attempted murder in four ways:

1. He lies in wait for his victim (substantial step).
2. He entices his victim to go to the location where the intended crime will take place.
3. He intentionally engages in criminal activity: he inflicts cuts on Cassio in an effort to kill him.
4. He knowingly engages in activities that help another commit a crime. He forces Emilia to steal Desdemona's handkerchief—a handkerchief that precipitates her murder by Othello.

Iago also commits first-degree murder—the premeditated killing of another human. Although premeditation denotes advance contemplation, the courts have ruled that such contemplation to engage in criminality need not take place over a period of time. One can premeditate instantaneously, just at the time when the crime is committed.

When the plot to kill Cassio is aborted, Iago immediately thinks of ways to cover up his involvement in it. Instantly, he plans how to murder Roderigo, the one person with knowledge of the crime. His actions—the numerous stabbings of Roderigo—adequately manifest his criminal intent.

Iago is a psychopath who revels in causing pain and suffering to others. His crimes are many and disgusting, and he sets out to accomplish them through a false aura of concern and through carefully crafted lies. First, he wins the trust and confidence of the people he plans to hurt, and then he perpetrates the evil. His victims have always thought well of him. Cassio, for instance, describes him as a man who "speaks home"; "of exceeding honesty"; "full of love and honesty." Othello says of him, "Iago is most honest." Iago is referred to as "honest" at least nine times in the play. For these reasons, it is understandable why Othello, Cassio, Roderigo, Emilia, and Desdemona all easily fall prey to his deceitful enterprises. As a murderer, Iago, by his own hands, kills two people; by sheer luck, his third victim escapes death. As a criminal who acts at the spur of the moment, Iago provokes the murder of Desdemona. Through persistent deception, he destroys a perfectly good marriage between Othello and Desdemona and brings about the firing of Cassio from his job. His craving for destruction is in large part not generated by what he believes would profit him but his desire to rob others of happiness.

His first murder victim, Roderigo, is a Venetian gentleman. Roderigo's murder was clearly a result of Iago's attempt to cover up his attempted murder of Cassio. Michael Cassio, who was Othello's lieutenant, occassionally played the role of a go-between in Othello's love affair with Desdemona. It is not therefore surprising that Desdemona and Othello developed a fondness toward Cassio. This friendship of the three, coupled with what Iago regarded as a slight when Cassio was promoted as Othello's general, led Iago to plot a horrid scheme of revenge that would involve Othello, Desdemona, Cassio, Emilia (Iago's wife), and Roderigo.

His first devilish act is to entice Cassio to drink heavily. When Cassio is drunk and starts a brawl, Othello fires him from the rank of general, just as Iago had hoped. Iago next lied to Roderigo, telling him that Othello had been assigned to Mauritania and that Cassio was to replace Othello as general in the Venetian army. The only way to prevent Cassio from taking over the position, as Iago explains to Roderigo, is by the "removing of Cassio" (IV.ii.245). When Roderigo demands a clarification of Iago's statement, Iago explains, "by making him uncapable of

Othello's place,—knocking out his brains" (IV.ii.247–48). Iago then lays out a plot to ambush Cassio. Cassio is to dine at a prostitute's in the night, and Iago will arrange for that meeting to be over between the hours of twelve and one. Thereafter, as Iago tells Roderigo,

> you may take him at your pleasure: I will be near to second your attempt, and he shall fall between us. Come, stand not amazed at it, but go along with me; I will show you such a necessity in his death that you shall think yourself bound to put it on him. (IV.ii.255–61)

The two meet and, following Iago's directives, they wait for Cassio at different posts. Iago justifies his action. He is indifferent to any potential harm to Roderigo (although he would want him live for selfish reasons):

> now whether he kill Cassio or Cassio him, or each do kill the other, every way makes my gain: live Roderigo, he calls me to a restitution large of gold and jewels that I bobb'd from him as gifts to Desdemona; it must not be: If Cassio do remain, he hath a daily beauty in his life that makes me ugly; and besides, the Moor may unfold me to him; there stand I in much peril: no he must die. (V.i.17–28)

Iago and Roderigo waylay Cassio. Roderigo "rushes out, and makes a pass at Cassio" (V.i.31). Cassio stabs and wounds Roderigo in the process. Iago "rushes from his post, cuts Cassio behind in the leg and exits" (V.i.37–38). Fortunately for Cassio, he eludes death. When he cries out for help, Iago, with an ulterior motive, is the first to arrive on the scene. Knowing exactly what he was doing and who he was attacking, Iago stabs and kills Roderigo. In order to absolve himself from culpability, he explains that he thought he was stabbing the thief who had injured Cassio. A note in Roderigo's pocket, however, revealed Iago's treachery.

Iago's diabolical acts extend to his wife, Emilia, a good but submissive woman. Iago calls her "a foolish wife" (III.iii.378). It is from Emilia that Iago (under a false pretext to duplicate the work) gets the handkerchief he uses to bring into question Desdemona's loyalty to Othello. After Iago persistently pressures her, she stealthily picks up a handkerchief Othello had given to Desdemona as a gift.

When Emilia vows to disclose the truth about Iago's role in Desdemona's death, Iago threatens then stabs her to death. "Come, hold your peace" (V.ii.289) Iago cautions Emilia, but she is too outraged to keep quiet. " 'Twill out, 'twill out," she exclaims. Again her husband advises, "[B]e wise, and get you home" (V.ii.290). When Emilia refuses to obey, Iago threatens to stab her. When Emilia at last tells Othello that Iago had begged her to steal the handkerchief, which was the proximate cause of Desdemona's murder, Iago inflicts abuses on her—"villanous whore!"; filth, thou liest" (V.ii.304, 307)—then stabs her and runs out.

In ending Emilia's life, Iago commits the following offenses: threats to commit bodily harm, inflicting deadly wounds with a weapon, and fleeing the scene of a crime.

CRIMINAL SOLICITATION: IAGO

The crime of solicitation requires that the architect of a criminal plot request or ask a third party to execute the criminal enterprise. The crime of solicitation was punishable at common law regardless of whether the person being enlisted undertook the criminal venture or not. The law treated those who urged others to commit misdemeanors in the same way as those who enlisted someone to commit a felony. The offense was punishable at common law as a misdemeanor, but in Shakespeare's time, it was treated more harshly to deter people from the soaring attractions of a life of crime.

The *Model Penal Code* (section 5.02) defines solicitation as follows:

> A person is guilty of solicitation to commit a crime if with purpose of promoting or facilitating its commission he commands, encourages or requests another person to engage in specific conduct which would constitute such crime or attempt to commit such crime or which would establish his complicity in its commission or attempted commission.

The motivations for recruiting another person to do the dirty work are open to conjecture. One can speculate that those who solicit others to commit crimes do so to shield their identity; or perhaps to have a more able person do the crime. Those who solicit may be intent on inducting others to share a life of crime with them. Perhaps they simply lack the courage to carry out the crime alone.

As the definition of solicitation suggests, what constitutes the guilty act are the words of the recruiter. Although words constitute the crime, courts are careful to decipher empty words not intended to have any binding effect from those that are intended to enlist the services of another. The courts require that the words offer some inducements. Words that "advise, command, counsel, encourage, entice, entreat, importune, incite, induce, instigate, procure, request, solicit, urge" make up the crime (Samaha 1996, p. 199). Words expressive of a specific criminal intent are tantamount to criminal solicitation.

Solicitations for criminal activity need not be scripted, but once the purpose of the recruiter is written, it is immaterial that the recipient never received the note. The crime of solicitation has occurred regardless. In addition, it is irrelevant if the third party refuses to participate in the crime; solicitation occurred anyway.

Iago committed another kind of abhorrent crime which could be classified as criminal solicitation. The statutory definition of criminal solicitation is that a person, with intent, causes another person to "engage in conduct constituting a crime the accused solicits, requests, commands, importunes or otherwise attempts to cause such other person to engage in such conduct" (Inbau et al. 1997, p. 525).

As can be inferred from his conduct, Iago solicits Othello to kill Desdemona to destroy Othello's own reputation by leading him into a life of criminality. Throughout much of the play, Iago enjoys the reputation of being an honest man. One can thus understand why he refrains from killing Desdemona himself but makes Othello do it.

Iago could not put behind him the fact that Othello had chosen Cassio over him to be his general. That slight, coupled with an unfounded suspicion that Othello had a special fondness for Emilia, Iago's wife, led Iago to seek revenge. Iago confides in Roderigo, "I hate the Moor: my cause is hearted" and, in a soliloquy shortly after, reaffirms his feelings and lays the scheme for his evil deeds:

> I hate the Moor; and it is thought abroad that 'twixt my sheets he has done my office: I know not if't be true; But I for mere suspicion in that kind, will do as if for surety. He holds me well; the better shall my purpose work on him. Cassio's a proper man: Let me see now; To get his place, and to plume up my will in double knavery,—How, how?—Let's see:—After some time to abuse Othello's ear that he is too familiar with his wife:—He hath a person and a smooth dispose, to be suspected; fram'd to make women false. The Moor is of a free and open nature, that thinks men honest that but seem to be so; and will as tenderly be led by the nose as asses are. I have't;—it is engender'd:—hell and night must bring this monstrous birth to the world's light. (I.iii.456–75)

The plan is laid out, the mind-set is established, and it can be only a matter of time before Iago's wishes are realized. Cassio, who had been fired from his job (by Iago's doing), turns to Iago for advice about how he can get back his job. Iago advises Cassio to ask Desdemona to mediate for him with Othello—good advice, if it had not been given for some devious purpose. Desdemona, not suspecting a setup, intercedes in Cassio's behalf. As Cassio leaves after a meeting with Desdemona, Iago, full of crafty devices, says in a low tone, "Ha! I like not that" (III.iii.37). As the conversation proceeds, Iago pretentiously exclaims, "indeed," at Othello's affirmation that Cassio had played the role of a middleman between him and Desdemona. The two statements made by Iago leave an indelible impression on Othello. Seeds of jealousy have been sowed in Othello's mind and he begins to suspect that Cassio is having an affair with his wife.

From that point onward, Iago never misses an opportunity to raise the level of suspicion in Othello's mind, and he does so while feigning concern for Othello. Iago tells Othello to be wary of Venetian women because "they do let heaven see the pranks they dare not show their husbands; their best conscience is not to leave undone, but keep unknown" (III.iii.252–55). "Beware of jealousy," he warns Othello but advises him to keep close watch over Cassio and Desdemona. Such mixed messages make Othello, who trusts Iago, even more suspicious. Othello says of Iago, "[T]his fellow's of exceeding honesty, and knows all quality, with a learned spirit, of human dealings" (III.iii.323).

Faking honesty, Iago pretends to be sorry for revealing to Othello what is going on, but he reminds Othello that Desdemona had turned down suitors of her own "clime and complexion" (III.iii.292), something that was not normally done, the drift being that she now wants someone of her race. When Othello takes Iago by the throat, demanding him to "prove [his] love a whore," Iago lies to Othello by telling him of Cassio's mutterings full of love for Desdemona in his sleep. He further tells Othello that "such a handkerchief I am sure it was your wife's,—did I today see Cassio wipe his beard with" (III.iii.535–37). Othello replies, "[I]f it be that . . . my bloody thoughts with violent pace, shall ne'er look back, ne'er ebb to humble love, till that a capable and wide revenge swallow them up" (III.iii.538, 560–63).

When Othello passes out, or "falls in a trance," from the grief he experiences as a result of firmly believing that Desdemona is unfaithful to him, Iago jubilates, "Work on, my medicine, work! thus credulous fools are caught; and many worthy and chaste dames even thus, all guiltless, meet reproach" (III.iv.59–62).

Step by step, as Othello plans the murder of Desdemona, Iago knows but does nothing to stop him. Finally, when Othello asks Iago for poison to get rid of Desdemona, Iago coldly suggests, "[D]o it not with poison, strangle her in her bed, even the bed she hath contaminated" (IV.i.250–51). Othello does just that.

SUMMARY

The crimes of murder, attempted murder, attempt at committing grievious bodily harm, criminal solicitation, and accessory before and after the fact form the basis of the discussion in this chapter. The murder (treason) of Duncan by Macbeth was committed in the hopes that Macbeth would become king. Macbeth's wife, Lady Macbeth, provided the needed reinforcements before and after the commission of the murder. Iago's crimes were committed out of sheer malevolence. Since he was a sadist, it was inconsequential to him how his devilish acts impacted others. Richard III at first committed murder to fulfill his quest for power. Unfortunately, even after he became king, his criminal ploys worsened as he engaged in a series of senseless killings. Othello committed murder because he was extremely gullible. Not suspecting that Iago was telling lies about Desdemona's infidelity, Othello killed a very fine lady. Shylock's crime was peculiar in the sense that it stemmed from an unconscionable transaction. An unsuspecting Shylock thought that it was acceptable to carve flesh from Antonio's chest, not knowing that his actions would be considered criminal.

4
Property Crimes

Robbery is defined as "felonious taking of money, personal property, or any other article of value, in the possession of another, from his person or immediate presence, and against his will, accomplished by means of force or fear" (Black 1990, p. 1329). Unlike theft, robbery entails the use of force or threatened force. Simply put, robbery is aggravated theft. The elements of robbery can be deduced from its definition:

Felonious taking

Carrying away (asportation)

Other's property

From their person or immediate presence

With force or threatened force

With intent to deprive permanently the rightful owner of the property.

It follows that to constitute a crime of robbery, an immediate threat of the use of force will suffice. Threats of the use of force on the victim's family and on the victim's place of abode may be sufficient. Threats to other kinds of property and to reputation may not qualify as threatened force.

Robbery may be classified into three degrees. Robbery in the first degree comprises the use of weapons, threatened use of weapons, and serious injury to the victim. Second-degree robbery entails the display of weapons, the use of accomplices, and the infliction of injuries. Third-degree robbery occurs when the pepertrator is unarmed but uses force or threatened force on the victim. Falstaff and his gang are accused of robbery because they use force and threats to dispossess the travelers of their goods.

ROBBERY: FALSTAFF

In *1 Henry IV*, Falstaff is described as a cheat, a drunk, a liar, and a robber, among other things. He himself confirms these descriptions in the opening scene of the play: "[W]e that take purses," "we steal," "squires of the night," "I am a villain" (I.ii.15, 33, 27, 110).

Falstaff and his friends are involved in a robbery in which the amount of approximately 3,000 marks is stolen. The gang lies in wait for their victims and then use force and intimidation to overcome the travelers' resistance to part with their property. Falstaff, the leader of the gang, commands them to "strike," "cut the villains' throats ... down with them, fleece them" (II.ii. 94–97). The travelers run off leaving behind their money. The crime of robbery is thus accomplished. Sufficient immediate threats of harm were made to the travelers.

EMBEZZLEMENT/MISAPPROPRIATION OF FUNDS: FALSTAFF

Misappropriation is the "unauthorized, improper, or unlawful use of funds or other property for purpose other than that for which intended" (Black 1990, p. 998). The crime of embezzlement and obtaining property by false pretense are governed in some jurisdictions under theft statutes. Typically, embezzlers do not take property because, in most cases, the property is already in their possession for a specified purpose. Since one cannot be charged with unlawful taking of what one possesses, embezzlers can be charged only with conversion. Embezzlers have a fiduciary relationship with the rightful owner of the property. They therefore acquire possession of the property because the rightful possessor establishes trust in them and thereby delegates them the use of the property for a specific purpose. When that trust is breached and the person with temporal possession converts the property for a purpose other than that specified, the person with temporal possession has committed a crime of embezzlement or misappropriation.

Falstaff does precisely this. As Prince Hal and his father, King Henry IV, prepare for a war against the Percys, Hal assigns Falstaff to be leader of the infantry. When apprised of his assignment, Falstaff wishes he was commander of troops on horses instead; that way he could use them for robberies: "I would it had been of horse. Where shall I find one that can steal well?" (III.iii.210–11).

Falstaff is instructed by Hal to meet with him the following day. Falstaff's responsibilities are explained to him, and the money to recruit and to equip his soldiers is given to him. "[M]eet me tomorrow in the Temple-hall . . . there shalt thou know thy charge, and there receive money and order for their furniture" (III.iii.223–26).

Falstaff, in a position of trust, misuses the power and the funds allocated to him. Instead of recruiting a capable and healthy army, he keeps the funds for himself and recruits men from off streets—a host of raggedy, infirm people. He himself acknowledges, "If I be not ashamed of my soldiers, I am a soused gurnet. I have misused the king's press damnably. I have got in exchange of a hundred and fifty soldiers, three hundred and odd pounds" (IV.ii.14–16).

THEFT/LARCENY: POMPEY

Theft is a common law crime against property. At some point in English history, thieves were sentenced to death when caught. The reason in part for such draconian punishment was to alleviate the swelling vagrant population. The material elements of larceny are as follows:

Wrongfully taking

Carrying away (asportation)

Of another's

Property

With the intent to deprive permanently the owner of the property.

In order to constitute a crime of theft, there has to be a taking of property either directly or indirectly. By direct taking, the thief actually lays hands on the object; by indirect taking, the thief dispenses of another's property without physically taking the thing. An example of indirect taking is selling a neighbor's puppy that strays into one's yard to someone else who picks up the puppy and departs with it. The seller never touches the puppy although he sells it to a buyer who picks it up and takes it away.

Stolen property has to move from its initial position. If a person has the mind-set to steal but does not move the property an inch from its original position, the person may not be considered to have stolen. The element of asportation has to be present along with other elements for a crime of larceny to occur.

Property that is considered stolen must be that of some other person. It follows that one cannot be accused of stealing something that one already possesses. The law distinguishes between possession and custody. Possession denotes "dominion and control." A person should be able to exercise a right and control over property for the property to be in that person's possession. Custody, on the other hand, relates to "keeping, guarding, care, watch, preservation" of something (see Gifis 1984, p. 113). To be a custodian of something does not give one the unfettered right to part with the thing without the permission of the rightful owner. Custodians who part with property in their custody can be charged with theft.

It is crucial, in a charge of theft, to show that a person who takes property illegally, or parts with property without rightful permission, intends to deprive the owner of possession permanently. With the advent of technology and more sophisticated transactions, theft now includes the taking of services and of tangible and intangible goods and intellectual property. This was not the case in the early centuries, when one could steal only tangible goods.

In *Measure for Measure*, Pompey, the clown, is a servant of the infamous Mistress Overdone, who opens another disorderly house after the former one has been closed down by force. Pompey, a dedicated employee of Mistress Overdone, sees no reason for the state to close down his employer's business. Pompey does nothing wrong directly, but he is in the service of a dishonorable trade. For that he is reprimanded, but he is later arrested for stealing a "picklock." Where, how, and from whom he stole the picklock are not disclosed. All that is mentioned in the play is that he was later arrested for stealing a picklock. For this latter offense, the Duke recommended that Pompey be incarcerated, otherwise he might become a habitual criminal.

SUMMARY

The property crimes discussed in this chapter are robbery, misappropriation, and theft. Falstaff and his gang lie in wait for travelers, use force to overcome them, and take away their money and belongings. Falstaff is also an embezzler. Instead of using funds entrusted to him for a specific reason, Falstaff uses the money for his own personal needs. Pompey, the clown, a devoted employee of Mistress Overdone, is arrested for petty larceny.

5

Noncriminal Deviance and Nonviolent Sexual Deviance

SUICIDE: LADY MACBETH

S. Gifis defines suicide as "the voluntary and intentional killing of one's self" (1984, p. 462). Common law considered suicide a felony, but because a deceased person cannot be punished, the law acted on the estate of the deceased. All of the deceased's possessions were usually confiscated by the sovereign. Attempted suicide was punished as a misdemeanor.

Contemporary statutes related to suicide make aiding and abetting suicide a crime, although one survey shows that two out of three Americans approve of euthanasia and physician-assisted suicide for vegetative and terminally ill patients (*New York Times*, November 4, 1991, p. 9). Michigan's Dr. Jack Kevorkian is widely known for his numerous assisted suicides. In 1994 the supreme court of Michigan held that assisted suicide was a common law crime. Kevorkian was jailed in 1992 for assisting in the suicide of a patient and again in 1993 after which he was put under house arrest. He has, on occasion, won lawsuits brought against him. On Sunday, November 21, 1998, CBS's *60 Minutes* aired a special showing Dr. Kevorkian injecting a patient, Thomas Youk, who had requested Kevorkian's assistance, with a lethal dose of poisons. Youk died almost immediately. A few days later, Kevorkian was charged with murder.

Dr. Kevorkian was found guilty and convicted of second degree murder, since he himself administered the lethal medicine to Youk. On April

13, 1999, after explaining to Dr. Kevorkian the importance of the rule of law, the judge sentenced him to 10–25 years in prison. Dr. Kevorkian plans to appeal (*The Lancet* 353, no. 9161 [April 17, 1999]: 1340).

After murdering Duncan, the Macbeths are haunted by guilt. Lady Macbeth lapses into a frenzy from which she never recovers. She is queen, and her husband is king as she had wished, but she soon realizes that they can never find peace of mind. She exclaims in sorrow, "[T]is safer to be that which we destroy, than, by destruction, dwell in doubtful joy" (III.ii.9–10). As Lady Macbeth watches her husband being afflicted by terrible dreams and languishing in "sorriest fancies," she is overwhelmed by misery. Her nights are marred by "slumbery agitation." At other times she acts strangely; for instance, she washes imaginary blood off her hands over and over again. Her whispers are full of guilty utterances, but she realizes that "what's done cannot be undone" (V.i.75). At the end, it is believed that Lady Macbeth "by self and violent hands took off her life" (V.viii.92–93).

Death by suicide and attempted suicide has been defined in various terms as criminal for many generations: sometimes it is considered a felony crime: sometimes, deviant behavior.

ALCOHOLISM: FALSTAFF

Black defines alcoholism as "the pathological effect (as distinguished from physiological effect) of excessive indulgence in intoxicating liquors" (1990, p. 70). Statutes against alcoholism and substance abuse are usually enacted to ensure that persons under the influence of any of these intoxicants do not disturb the public peace by posing threats to themselves, to others, or to property. Although the sale of alcohol is not prohibited (except to minors and after certain hours of the day), it is the activities of those who get drunk in public places that give rise to the legislation pertinent to this discussion. Public drunkenness is more likely to be manifested by those with no stake in society. Indeed, the 1967 President's Commission on Law Enforcement and Administration of Justice in the United States revealed that a good number of people arrested for being drunk in public places are "homeless, penniless, and beset with acute personal problems" (p. 233).

Although alcoholism may be a disease, a drunk may still be punished for getting drunk in a public place. The U.S. Supreme Court made it clear in the case of *Powell v. Texas* (1968) that the act of being drunk in a public place was punishable since it offended public decency. Powell was not punished for the condition or status of being an alcoholic; he was punished for being drunk in public. The Court contrasted the *Powell* decision with its earlier decision in *Robinson v. California* (1962). In *Robinson*, the Court held that it is cruel and unusual to punish someone for the condition or illness of drug addiction. Although both Powell and Robinson were sick, the distinction is that Powell got drunk in the public where he could become a danger to passersby, himself, and property.

A person who voluntarily intoxicates himself or herself may not be excused from criminal liability. Voluntary intoxication can only negate *mens rea* (the guilty mind) and thus reduce the charges against a person. Involuntary intoxication (that is, when a person did not know he or she was taking intoxicants) may excuse criminal liability.

Alcoholism has been a problem from time immemorial, and in early modern England, it was even more prevalent (see Beier 1985; Sharpe 1984; Salgado 1977). Alehouses were breeding grounds not just for alcoholics, but also for all kinds of degenerative behavior.

> At the ale-house the idle meet to game and quarrel; here the gamblers form their stratagems; here the pick-pockets hide themselves till dusk, and gangs of thieves form their plots and routs; here conspirators contrive their hellish devices; and here the combinations of journeymen are made to execute their silly schemes. (J. Fielding 1758, quoted in Sharpe 1984, p. 104)

The offense of drunkenness in public has never been punished severely except during a serious disturbance of the peace or, worse, if the offender drives a vehicle while under the influence of alcohol.

Falstaff's offense relates to drunkenness in a public place, an offense against public morals. Falstaff is an idler who engages in too much drinking. When he is introduced in *1 Henry IV*, he is just waking up after too much drink. "What time of day is it lad?" he asks Prince Hal. Hal responds, "Thou art so fat-witted with drinking of old sack . . . to demand that truly which thou wouldst truly know" (I.ii.1–6). After the robbery occurs at Gadshill, Falstaff drinks so heavily that when he is told to hide behind the arras so he is not apprehended by police, he falls sound asleep. From his pocket a receipt is taken which shows that Falstaff spends most of his money on "sack" and very little on food. Throughout the play, mention is made of his drinking habits. He ingests more alcohol than food, and he owes the tavern money for drinks he takes on credit. These habits, in addition to stealing to purchase liquor, are symptoms of alcoholism.

VAGRANCY: FROTH

A vagrant is a person who "wanders from place to place, one who has no settled habitation, nor any fixed income or livelihood" (Black 1990, p. 1548). In early modern England, vagrants permeated not only the big cities but also the countryside. Some were forced into an idle life as a result of economic, social, demographic, and political factors; others reveled in laziness simply because they enjoyed the low life of begging.

At some point in time, when the growth of vagrants equaled the rate of growth of the population, government increased attempts to ameliorate the problem (Beier 1985). Vagrants were classified in several different categories: pedlars, tinkers, discharged soldiers, students, wizards and witches, soothsayers, and unlicensed healers. Legislation to address the problem varied. In 1576 houses of corrections were opened to confine vagrant youths. While they lived in those houses, they were subjected to harsh labor and were taught work ethics so that they could obtain jobs after release. Between 1572 and 1597, vagrants between the ages of five and fourteen were locked up and whipped; those over fourteen were whipped and burned in the ear. In 1597 those under the age of seven were no longer prosecuted.

Poor Laws were enacted to regulate begging and other types of vagrancy. Beggars were whipped, branded, or incarcerated. A vagrant who had already served time in prison was required by a 1597 law to have in his possession a document that indicated his birth place, previous address, and destination, as well as certification of time already served. Exactly who was a vagrant was not really clear; the keepers of the peace usually made that determination.

The problem with regard to statutes that deal with vagrancy in the United States is that many of them are so broad that they encompass constitutionally protected behavior. Based on their discretion, police officers can arrest anyone who they think is a vagrant. Many such statutes have been ruled void for being too inclusive or being too vague because they are not precise as to the specific behavior they prohibit.

Vagrancy laws were introduced to the United States through the 1714 English Vagrancy Act. This law distinguished three categories of vagrants: rogues and vagabonds, incorrigible rogues, and idle and disorderly people. The *Model Penal Code* lists the following as crimes of vagrancy:

Person living in idleness without employment or visible means of support

Common prostitute

Common drunkard

Common gambler

Keeper of a house of prostitution

Keeper of a house of gambling

Wanton, dissolute, or lascivious person

Associate of known thieves.

In *Papachristou v. City of Jacksonville*, 405 U.S. 156 (1972), the U.S. Supreme Court ruled against a vagrancy ordinance that did not clearly define prohibited behavior. The Court has made it clear that laws should be written in precise and certain language so that peoples' constitutionally protected rights cannot be arbitrarily infringed by law enforcement officials. States vary in the wordings of their vagrancy or loitering statutes. Where the statutes are clearly worded, those who infringe on them are punished accordingly.

Froth, in *Measure for Measure*, is a vagrant, "a foolish gentleman," who frequents Mistress Overdone's disorderly house for no apparent purpose. Froth is not vicious and commits no crime; however, his status as a tramp is deviant and socially undesirable. The state would rather have him lead a decent and productive life.

Froth and Pompey are arrested by constable Elbow who refers to them as "notorious benefactors" (II.i.60). In his briefing of Angelo about the two deviants, Elbow says the two are "precise villains...void of all profanation in the world that good Christians ought to have" (II.i.64–67). Froth and Pompey, as is obvious from their diction, have very limited, if any, education.

NONVIOLENT SEXUAL DEVIANCE: FORNICATION/ SOCIAL CORRUPTION: ANGELO

In modern times, fornication is classified as an offense against public morals. It is defined as "sexual intercourse other than between married persons" (Black 1990, p. 653), although it is not uncommon to find it defined differently by different state statutes.

Although fornication relates to sexual activities between consenting adults, it has been regarded as indecent behavior throughout history. At some point in history, the offense fell under the domain of ecclesiastical settings. Some believe fornication should be classified as a criminal activity when one or both partners are married to someone else (adultery). Others believe that it is a moral issue which should be left to the conscience of the parties involved, and to their God. Since fornication does not entail coercion or violence, those involved may be fined small amounts of money and jailed for not more than six months. Fornication is not commonly punished especially when the two unmarried consenting adults carry on the activities behind closed doors. It is sometimes referred to as a victimless offense because it is a consensual activity and there is no complaining party. Other sexual activities that fall under public morals offenses are adultery, sodomy, indecent exposure, and prostitution.

In Shakespearean times, fornication fell under the realm of the monarchs and was thus criminalized as a move to cleanse the decaying morals of the people, but whose morals typified decent standards? *Measure for Measure*, in a sense, is a satire that depicts the problem of selecting another human to enforce some moral standards.

Angelo is the strict deputy delegated to cleanse Vienna of lechery. He is shrewd in the application of justice. So firm is his belief in justice that he proclaims, "[W]hen I, that censure him, do so offend, let mine own judgment pattern out my death, and nothing come partial" (II.i.37–39).

Contrary to his proclamations of uprightness, Angelo commits a series of infractions: fornication, sexual solicitation, abuse of public trust, and breach of promise. In his capacity as interim duke, Angelo sentences Claudio to death for the crime of fornication. Isabella, Claudio's sister, meets with Angelo to intercede on her brother's behalf. Her presence mesmerizes Angelo ("This virtuous maid subdues me quite") (II.ii.235–36), and he proposes a ransom for Claudio. Isabella is to offer him sexual gratification in exchange for Claudio's life: "[L]ay down the treasures of your body to this suppos'd, or else let him [Claudio] suffer" (II.vi.113–14). "We are all frail" (II.vi.140), Angelo acknowledges, but he will not forgive Claudio's frailty. Isabella rejects the proposal and threatens to make it public. Angelo assumes that because of his "unsoil'd name, the austereness of [his] life, [his] place i'the state," no one will believe Isabella (II.iv.183). Angelo has ample time to recant his desire; instead, he sets a meeting for the act to be consummated and then designs ways to cover up the offense. Hence, while Claudio's offense is spontaneous, Angelo's offense is premeditated.

Angelo gets what he wants—sex albeit with the wrong woman—but he fails to fulfill his own part of the bargain. He sends an order for Claudio to be beheaded before dawn, and to make sure his order is carried out, he asks for Claudio's head. He breaches the agreement with Isabella because, as he says, "[T]he riotous youth, with dangerous sense, might in the times to come have ta'en revenge, by receiving a dishonour'd life with ransom of such shame" (IV.iv.35–38). Angelo, therefore, breaks the law after careful consideration of his actions. His crime is not as spontaneous as Claudio's.

The "austere" Angelo has other blemishes in his character; he is mean and inconsiderate. He broke his engagement to Mariana when the dowry Mariana was to have given him was destroyed in a shipwreck.

FORNICATION: CLAUDIO

In Shakespeare's time, fornication was a crime punishable by death. Claudio is sentenced to die for engaging in sexual intercourse with his fiancée, whom he impregnated. The act was perfectly mutual, according to his fiancée, Juliet; but this fact does not suffice as grounds for mitigation. Claudio still faces the death penalty. Claudio's offense, arising out of a gust of passion with his betrothed, is spontaneous. He nonetheless broke the law because Viennese law did not allow sex between unmarried people.

SUMMARY

Offenses in this chapter are discussed under two broad categories. The first category is noncriminal deviance, which includes suicide, alcoholism, and vagrancy. Lady Macbeth commits suicide when she can no longer bear the guilt of her role in the murder of Duncan. In addition to his many other shortcomings, Falstaff is an alcoholic who borrows and steals to sustain his drinking problem. Froth is not accused of any crime; however, because he has no discernible purpose in life, he is arrested by constable Elbow.

The second category includes nonviolent sexual deviance. Two types of fornicators are discussed. Claudio, whose offense is venial, engages in premarital sex with his betrothed. For this offense, he is sentenced to death. Angelo, the deputy who sentences Claudio to death, solicits sex in exchange for a commutation of the death sentence against Claudio. Whereas Claudio's offense is spontaneous, Angelo's is premeditated and intended to foster corruption.

PART III

RELATIONSHIP BETWEEN CRIMINOLOGICAL THEORY AND THE BEHAVIOR OF SELECTED SHAKESPEAREAN CHARACTERS

INTRODUCTION

Part III, which discusses motivations for criminal and deviant behavior, also analyzes Shakespeare's possible interpretations of why his characters deviate from conventional behavior. Established criminological theories are introduced and related to Shakespeare's commentary on crime. The intent of this part is not to test theories; rather, it is to link Shakespeare's ideas to contemporary criminological thinking. It is not presumed that all theories of crime can be found in the sample of plays in this book. This study demonstrates that, from a representative sample of Shakespearean plays, substantial illustrations of the Bard's legal and criminological orientations are very evident.

Twelve criminological theories and perspectives are discussed in nine separate chapters. In this conjunction, the underlying motivation for the antisocial behavior of Shakespeare's characters, most of which was discussed in chapters 3, 4, and 5, are outlined. Where appropriate, some characters are discussed jointly; if a particular theory can be explained and exemplified by more than one character, those characters are discussed in the same chapter to avoid redundancy. When more than one theory can be applied to explain a character's behavior, the discussion is presented in separate chapters.

Instead of completely discussing a particular character before another is introduced, the analysis employs an approach wherein a Shakespearean character is introduced along with the character's behavior as that behavior exemplifies a particular theoretical perspective in criminology. This complies with conventional theoretical ordering. It is tedious and pointless to analyze each character separately. Not only are fewer theories deduced in some plays than in others, but also the variables that explain the theories may be fewer.

WHAT IS A THEORY?

In discussing the meaning of criminological "theory," R. Akers states that a well-developed theory is concerned with "real situations, feelings, experience, and human behavior" (1997, p. 1). Although criminological theories are abstract, as he states, they usually have more substance about human behavior than mere speculations. Three definitions of theories are adopted from Akers here:

1. In general, scientific theories make statements about the relationship between two classes of phenomena (Vold and Bernard 1986, p. 4).

2. Theories are generalizations of a sort; they explain how two or more events are related to each other (Williams and McShane 1988, p. 2).

3. A theory is a set of interconnected statements or propositions that explain how two or more events or factors are related to one another (Curran and Renzetti 1994, p. 2).

According to T. J. Bernard, all theory must be based on research, "even if empirical observations are scattered . . . and crude." Science, he notes, only "progresses through careful alternation between theory and research. . . . Theory interprets the results of past research and charts the direction of future research" (Bernard 1990, pp. 329–30).

In order to know whether a theory offers a good explanation of crime or criminal justice, the following ingredients, among others, must be included in the theory:

1. Logical consistency, scope, and parsimony: The concepts must be clearly defined and its propositions log-

ically stated, and they must be internally consistent. The scope of a theory pertains to the purview of the phenomena it intends to explain. A parsimonious theory is one that adopts the simplest set of concepts and propositions (Akers 1997, pp. 6–7).

2. Testability: A scientific theory must be testable objectively, and repeatedly tested empirically (1997, p. 7).

3. Empirical validity: A theory must be supported by research evidence (p. 9).

4. Empirical validity and the concept of causality and determinism: A theory must have specified variables that precede the occurrence of the antisocial behavior, and they must help predict when the behavior will occur or recur (p. 10).

5. Usefulness and policy implications: A good theory provides guidelines for social and criminal justice policy (p. 11).

Table 2
Theories of Crime and Corresponding Characters Implied or Stated in the Plays

Theory	Crime	Character	Play
Classicalism/rational choice	Murder	Macbeth	*Macbeth*
Lombrosianism	Murder	Richard III	*Richard III*
Theories of heredity	Murder	Richard III	*Richard III*
Psychopathy and the antisocial personality	Murder and criminal solicitation	Iago	*Othello*
Ecological theory	Theft	Pompey	*Measure for Measure*
	Vagrancy	Froth	*Measure for Measure*
Social learning theories			
Differential association	Murder	Othello	*Othello*
Social learning theory	Murder	Richard III	*Richard III*
Social control and bond theories			
Techniques of neutralization/drift	Accessory before and after the fact	Lady Macbeth	*Macbeth*
Social bond theory	Murder	Othello	*Othello*
	Murder	Richard III	*Richard III*
Normalcy of crime	Criminal solicitation	Iago	*Othello*
	Fornication	Angelo	*Measure for Measure*
	Fornication	Claudio	*Measure for Measure*

Table 2
Continued

Theory	Crime	Character	Play
Strain/anomie theory	Robbery	Falstaff	*1 Henry IV*
	Theft	Pompey	*Measure for Measure*
	Vagrancy	Froth	*Measure for Measure*
Social reaction/labeling theory	Attempt at committing grievous bodily harm	Shylock	*The Merchant of Venice*
Conflict theory	Attempt at committing grievous bodily harm	Shylock	*The Merchant of Venice*
Integrated theories			
Pathways in the life course to crime	Murder	Richard III	*Richard III*
Interactional theory of delinquency	Murder	Richard III	*Richard III*

6

Classicalism: Rational Choice: Macbeth

In the eighteenth century, two notable classicalists, Jeremy Bentham and Cesare Beccaria, examined social conditions and their influence on human behavior. The following three ideas are derived from their findings: (1) People are rational beings free to choose their cause of action. (2) In order to prevent or control crime, punishment must be severe, certain, and swift. This idea stems from the conviction that when a legal system does not enforce the law consistently, uniformly, and swiftly, the expected pain of crime (which is punishment) is minimized. Lawbreakers are thus more likely to capitalize on the benefits of crime. A legal system that is reduced to lawlessness is likely to be incapable of curbing crime (Akers 1997, p. 16). (3) Punishment is inherently evil and should only be used for deterrence (Akers 1994, pp. 49–51). The concept of deterrence takes two forms: specific deterrence (special deterrence) and general deterrence. Specific deterrence renders the offender incapable of furthering his criminal activities (at least, that is the intent). General deterrence is intended to discourage the rest of society from committing crimes through threats of sanctions. This school of thought assumes that crime is a consequence of painless shortcuts to success. That is, humans are rational and intelligent and are able to find an easier way to achieve their needs even if that way is deviant. Crime, according to this school of thought, is committed by an individual who, after assessing the likely benefits of the act against the cost of it, engages in the act because of the expected benefit. Therefore, crime is the free choice of a person. Humans do things which they believe serves them some good.

Shakespeare, writing centuries earlier, held the perspective that humans have free will to make rational choices and sometimes exercise this choice to do things that are socially inappropriate. Macbeth's character illustrates this viewpoint. After Macbeth demonstrates his valor in the Scottish war against the Norwegians, the king rewards him with a promotion from general to Thane of Cawdor. This comes to Macbeth as a surprise, even though the witches predicted this promotion, because the current Thane of Cawdor is still alive. If he can be Thane of Glamis, and Thane of Cawdor as the witches predicted, Macbeth is certain he can be king as well: "Two truths are told as the swelling act of the imperial theme" (I.iii.137–39).

Macbeth fails to realize that he has become Thane of Cawdor through his hard work and perhaps, by working harder, he can rise farther. Instead, he seeks shortcuts to greatness. Even with a promise of further promotions from the king—"I have begun to plant thee, and will labour to make thee full of growing" (I.iv.33–34)—Macbeth does not reconsider his options. He could continue to work hard (that is, accept pain) and ascend the ladder of success through socially approved ways, or he could "avoid pain" by replacing the incumbent king through deviant ways. Macbeth chooses the latter path. Step after step, as Macbeth contemplates the crime, he is of rational mind and has the choice to avert the plot, but he goes ahead and kills the king regardless. Macbeth is aware of the wrongness of his choice, but at this point crime is more attractive; it is the path to success: "I have no spur to prick the sides of my intent, but only vaulting ambition which o'er leaps itself, and falls on the other" (I.vii.25–27).

Macbeth's character thus establishes the point that Shakespeare considered humans to be rational beings who, by their own free will, could choose crime as a means to meet their ends. After weighing the potential benefit to him of killing the king (i.e., becoming king himself), Macbeth with clear knowledge of the consequences of his action murders the king. This perspective discounts the notion that people are driven to commit crime by demons or some sickness. Furthermore, it counters the "deterministic" perspective that criminal behavior is generated by individuals and social factors beyond the control of the criminal. The rational/free choice perspective suggests that each person is master of his or her destiny, and each person must be held accountable for his or her actions. Stated differently, every thing we do, think, or fail to do is dependent on our wishes.

In explaining rational choice theory, F. Cullen and R. Agnew make the point that the theory does not maintain that those who break the law are completely rational (1999, p. 24). Rather, as they suggest, the theory assumes that deviants usually give some thought to the "costs and benefits" of the crime even though such thought may have been given hastily based on partial or incorrect information. This point seems to be relevant to the discussion of Macbeth. Although Macbeth clearly knew what he was doing when he stabbed the king to death, the witches' predictions, on which he relied, were at best partial. All they predicted was that Macbeth would be king; they did not predict how dreary Macbeth's efforts to ascend the throne and to solidify his power would be.

The benefits of crime may be pecuniary or nonmonetary (Cullen and Agnew 1999, p. 248). Macbeth's benefit was the throne. The cost of crime may comprise penalties instituted by the state (for example, fines, incarceration, intermediate sanctions, and death) or it may comprise informal social control (for instance, dismissal from job, revocation of title, lowering of rank, and much more). The cost of crime may also include "moral costs," for example, the guilt felt by a person who violates the law (1999, p. 248). Before Macbeth is killed, he experienced terrible bouts of guilt. It is the guilt, "the moral cost" of their crimes, that led Lady Macbeth to commit suicide.

SUMMARY

Macbeth epitomizes the human quest to succeed without exerting much effort. The normal route to become king, if not by lineage, was to earn it. This route required too much time and effort for Macbeth who, with the reinforcement of his wife, became power hungry. Knowing full well what was right and wrong, he clearly chose, with a rational mind, the way of violence.

The rational choice theorists contend that criminal behavior is the choice of the criminal. Each person is aware of the difference between right and wrong; therefore, the will to refrain from criminal behavior rests on each person.

7

Lombrosianism, Theories of Heredity, and Psychopathy and the Antisocial Personality

LOMBROSIANISM: RICHARD III

When Cesare Lombroso stated his theory of crime in 1863, based on the biological peculiarities of a person, he was not stating anything new. In his portrayal of Richard III, Shakespeare depicted Richard as a person who was poorly adjusted emotionally as a result of a significant deformity. Because of his poor adjustment, and triggered by constant reminders of his deformity, Richard learned to vent his anger through socially unacceptable ways.

According to Schafer, in Lombroso's theory,

A criminal is in a biologically separate category from other human beings. The criminal is, partly or totally, an abnormal organism, and this determines or at least largely motivates his criminal behavior. Thus the criminal is a biological anomaly whose criminal conduct originates in his somatic or psychic abnormalities. (1969, p. 183)

Lombroso considered these "abnormal organisms" (atavists) throwbacks from some crude civilization. In order to derive his theory of the "born criminal," Lombroso studied body types of Italian prisoners and compared them to those of Italian soldiers. Based on these comparisons, he concluded that, because the body parts of prisoners were different from those of people who conform to the law, the biological differences typical in prisoners cause them to break the law. Although Lombroso's conviction on the born criminal was unwavering, he nonetheless conceded that social, economic, and political conditions might also be instrumental in crime causation (Akers 1997, p. 37).

In as much as early biological theories have been criticized for their "simplistic" stance, recently more focus has been given to biological studies that relate to "genes, brain, central and autonomic nervous systems, nutrition, hormonal (male and female) balances, metabolism, physiological arousal levels, and biological processes in learning" (Akers 1997, p. 42). Modern biological theorists propose that social and environmental conditions enhance the biological traits that trigger criminal behavior. In essence, as D. Fishbein suggests, behavior is not inherited; how we respond to social and environmental stimuli denotes behavior.

> As a rule, what is inherited is not a behavior; rather it is the way in which an individual responds to the environment. It provides an orientation, predisposition, or tendency to behave in a certain fashion. . . . Findings of biological involvement in antisocial behavior have, in a few studies, disclosed measurable abnormalities, but in a number of studies, measurements do not reach pathologic levels. In other words . . . the biological values do not necessarily exceed normal limits and would not alarm a practicising physician. (Fishbein 1990, pp. 42, 54)

One can fully understand how Richard's deformity created the rage in him only by tracing his character to earlier plays. In *2 Henry VI*, one learns about Richard's deformity from Clifford's insults: "[H]ence heap of wrath, foul indigested lump, as crooked in thy manners as thy shape!" (V.i.185–87). Richard is further offended when called a "foul stigmatic." Richard's angered response bears undertones of impending evil: "[I]f not in heaven, you'll surely sup in hell" (V.i.256–57). These insults on his physical makeup leave Richard with a sense of inadequacy and bitterness. It is this bitterness that leads him to react violently toward people.

In *3 Henry VI*, Queen Margarate, who is insensitive to Richard's condition, derides him: "[B]ut thou art neither like thy sire nor dam; but like a foul misshapen stigmatic, mark'd by the destinies to be avoided, as venom toads, or lizards' dreadful stings" (II.ii.136–38). Richard is quick to flare up at these insults: "Iron of Naples hid with English gilt, whose father bears the title of a king . . . as if a channel should be call'd the sea, sham'st thou not, knowing whence thou art extraught, to let thy tongue detect thy base-born heart?" (II.ii.139–44). Toward the end of this play, through insults, King Henry reminds Richard of his unfortunate birth: "Thy mother felt more than a mother's pain, and yet brought forth less than a mother's hope, to wit,—an indigest deformed lump. . . . Teeth hadst thou in thy head when thou wast born, to signify thou cam'st to bite the world" (V.vi.64–66). Richard was deeply angered: "I'll hear no more, die prophet in thy speech" (V.vi.69–70), he tells the king and then stabs and kills him.

These insults about his deformity haunt Richard throughout his life. Sometimes he bears the insults calmly, as when Princess Anne describes him, among other things, as a "lump of foul deformity" (*Richard III*, I.ii.64), but for the most part, the insults make him bitter and full of vengeance and irritate his emotional sensitivity to his biological deficiency.

At the beginning of *Richard III*, Richard, in a monologue, tells us of his miseries, his jealousies, and his plans:

> I that am not shap'd for sportive tricks nor made to court an amorous looking-glass . . . cheated of feature by dissembling nature, deform'd, unfinished, sent before my time. . . . Since I cannot prove a lover . . . I am determined to prove a villain. (I.i.16–17, 22–23, 31, 33)

In brief, the born criminal is destined to criminality. Each time the born criminal is reminded of his or her misery, it is likely that, because of emotional maladjustment, the response will be inappropriate. As Akers suggests, current biological theories include the interaction of "biological, social, and psychological variables in crime and delinquency" (1997, p. 35). It becomes inevitable that any of these variables, when combined with the traits of a born criminal, will trigger an "aggressive response."

The insults about his deformity make Richard feel inadequate and angry. In order to prove to others that he can dominate them, Richard takes the path of violence. He kills not only because he wants to be king, but in large measure because he wants to prove that he is one to be feared and respected. This antisocial reaction is not caused by Richard's deformity; it is a result of the insults heaped on him because of the deformity.

Shakespeare's Richard III is a perfect example of the criminological phenomenon that explains criminal behavior through the interaction of biological, social, and psychological variables. Although there have been many debates about the importance of biological theories of crime (Katz and Chambliss 1995; Vold and Bernard 1986), Cullen and Agnew believe that "biological and psychological factors play at least some role in the generation of some crime—and that such factors may be especially important in understanding the behavior of chronic offenders" (1999, p. 2).

THEORIES OF HEREDITY: RICHARD III

R. Dugdale (1910) and H. Goddard (1927) traced the lineage of families presumed to have had a history of criminality in order to find out if criminals were born with that trait. In Dugdale's study, for instance, more than 50 percent of 1,000 descendants in the Jukes family were either criminals or deviants. It was concluded that certain biological traits associated with crime causation could be inherited by the descendants of a family. This once popular theory was discounted by later, more scientifically acceptable sociological theories. Nevertheless, a few researchers continue to pursue the so-called family tree studies.

Among the more current studies on heredity, the best known is that of Sarnoff Mednick of Denmark (1977) (see Akers 1994, pp. 79–80). Through research, Mednick tried to form a connection between the criminal tendencies of biological fathers with those of their sons raised by adoptive parents in Copenhagen, Denmark. Based upon his findings, he concluded that criminality was higher among sons whose biological and adoptive fathers had been criminals. Those sons whose biological fathers were criminals were more inclined to be criminals than if only their adoptive parents were criminals. Mednick subsequently conducted a similar study with a sample drawn from throughout Denmark. His findings confirmed those of the Copenhagen study. Mednick's theory of heredity, however, has been criticized for its limitations. It has not been replicated. Although his second study was conducted in an attempt to replicate the first, different variables were introduced. Therefore, it cannot be said that his initial study, based on a sample obtained exclusively from Copenhagen, was replicated.

According to his theory,

> Some genetic factor(s) is passed along from parent to offspring. Criminal or delinquent behavior is not directly inherited, nor does the genetic factor directly cause the behavior; rather, one inherits a greater susceptibility to succumb to criminogenic environments or to adapt to normal environments in a deviant way. (Akers 1997, p. 45)

Akers explains that Mednick's theory means that people who are likely to deviate inherit an autonomous nervous system (ANS) which is slower to respond to stimuli. He further states that people who inherit the slower trait are also slow or incapable of controlling deviant urges. Therefore, they are more likely to break the law (Akers 1997, p. 45).

Mednick's line of reasoning is evident in Shakespeare's writings. Richard's grandfather, the Earl of Cambridge, was a criminal who was charged with high treason against King Henry V and executed for this crime. Richard's father, the Duke of York, also engaged in a series of conspiracies to overthrow the king in order to claim the throne he believed was rightly his. In *3 Henry VI*, the Duke of York's party plot to overthrow the king. Throughout the process, Richard is made an integral part of the conspiracy. Not only is Richard made to believe that he is an heir apparent, he is also made to appreciate violence as a means to settle disputes. He not only witnesses violence, he is also initiated into it. It is no wonder that, throughout his life, Richard regards violence as normal behavior, even after he acquires the throne and has nothing more to fight for.

Put simply, Shakespeare proposes, through Richard III, that if parents engage in socially unacceptable behavior their offspring are more likely to yield to that kind of behavior even when placed in a more peaceful environment. The theory of heredity, as G. Vold and T. Bernard state, is based on the "commonsense observation that children tend to resemble their parents in appearance, mannerisms, and disposition" (1986, p. 85). Consequently, since Richard's father and grandfather were criminals, Richard inherited a criminal disposition from them. The frequent interaction between a parent and child may lead to the child's adopting the parent's mannerisms and other modes of behavior. Richard's father had adopted his own father's way of behaving, and Richard inherited his father's mannerisms.

PSYCHOPATHY AND THE ANTISOCIAL PERSONALITY: IAGO

In this section, an examination of viewpoints that explain deviant behavior on the basis of the personality traits of the individual is made. The ideas in this section spring from the psychological and psychiatric theories that maintain that criminal dispositions originate mainly in the personality of the offender. According to Vold and Bernard, the term personality "refers to the complex set of emotional and behavioral attributes that tend to remain relatively constant as the individual moves from situation to situation" (1986, p. 108). This section, therefore, is based on a discussion of Iago's behavioral attributes which are displayed toward the people with whom he is associated. The analysis relies on the psychiatric discussion of psychopathy, sociopathy, and the antisocial personality.

Contemporary notions of the sociopath originated with J. Koch, a German psychiatrist, who referred to antisocial traits as "psychopathic inferiority" instead of "moral insanity" as it was hitherto known (Bartol 1991, p. 59). In 1970 Robert Hare distinguished three types of psychopaths: (1) primary, (2) secondary or neurotic, and (3) dys-social. The secondary and dys-social psychopaths have violent and aggressive tendencies. The primary psychopaths, on the other hand, according to C. Bartol,

> are *usually* not volcanically explosive, violent, or extremely destruc-
> tive. They are more apt to be outgoing, charming, and verbally
> proficient. They may be criminals—in fact, in general they run in
> perpetual opposition to the law—but many are not. (1991, p. 61)

The *Diagnostic and Statistical Manual of Mental Disorders* (1986) defines the antisocial personality as follows:

> The term is reserved for individuals who are basically unsocialized
> and whose behavior pattern brings them repeatedly into conflicts
> with society. They are incapable of significant loyalty to individu-
> als, groups, or social values. They are grossly selfish, callous, irre-
> sponsible, impulsive, and unable to feel guilt or to learn from
> experience and punishment. Frustration tolerance is low. They tend
> to blame others or offer plausible rationalization for their behavior.
> (quoted in Vold and Bernard 1986, p. 122)

Vold and Bernard explain that the terms psychopath and sociopath "are not merely descriptions of behavior patterns but also imply that those behaviors originate in the personality of the individual" (1986, pp. 122–23). Akers explains that personality theory perceives criminal behavior as an expression of "sensation-seeking, rebelliousness, hostility, and so on" (1997, p. 53). He further explains that a psychopath is

> a self-centered person who has not been properly socialized into
> pro-social attitudes and values, who has developed no sense of
> right and wrong, who has no empathy with others, and who is
> incapable of feeling remorse or guilt for misconduct or harm to
> others. (1997, p. 54)

Shakespeare clearly depicted the personality traits explained in the definition above in the character of Iago in *Othello*. More explicitly, Shakespeare realized that Iago was incapable of feeling guilt or remorse over his actions, and because it was inconsequential to him what the outcome of his acts might be, he could commit any kind of crime.

Although Iago had cause for complaint for not having been preferred for the lieutenancy position, that fact, nor any other, justifies his crimes. His psychological makeup is such that he takes delight in seeing people suffer, and it is immaterial to him if they have done him no wrong. He wants Brabantio, Desdemona's father, for instance, to suffer for no ap-parent reason: "[A]nd though he in a fertile climate dwell, plague him with flies: though that his joy be joy, yet throw such changes of vexation on't, as it may lose some colour" (I.i.90–94). As for Othello, Iago is out-spoken about his hatred for him. Twice in a short conversation with Roderigo, Iago resonates the point, "I hate the Moor; my cause is hearted . . . let us be conjunctive in our revenge against him" (I.iii.441–42, 443–44). He plans to torment Othello emotionally so that Othello should kill his wife and destroy himself: "[I'll] put the Moor at jealousy so strong that judgment cannot cure" (II.i.361–63).

Iago has cruel thoughts about Cassio as well: "Cassio's a proper man: let me see now; to get his place, and to plume up my will in double knavery" (I.iii.463–65). He causes Cassio's dismissal from his position as lieutenant and then attempts to murder him. He does not express hatred toward Desdemona; however, he piles up false accusations to arouse Othello's jealousy resulting in her murder. Iago murders Roderigo, his ally, to silence him from revealing their attempt to kill Cassio. He kills his wife because she exposes the truth about Desdemona's handkerchief.

At every stage, Iago displays antisocial behavior. In his encounters with others, he does something criminal in order to make them suffer. This behavioral trait, as psychologists are likely to explain, originates in the personality of Iago. Bartol, in commenting about psychologists and sociologists who analyze criminal behavior, poses the question, "Which is more important in criminal activity, the person or the situation?" (1980, p. 5). Vold and Bernard are of the opinion that both the person and the situation are responsible for criminal activity (1986, p. 128). They explain that sometimes one's personality is the "major determinant of whether or not a person engages in criminal action, while in other cases the situation might exert the more powerful influence" (1986, p. 128). From reviewing Iago's behavior, the answer to Bartol's question seems to be the person. In all his crimes, Iago creates the situation directly or through trickery. Moreover, when he has the chance to avert the wrong, he does not do it; instead, he promotes it. He leads Othello on to kill Desdemona. Some contemporary researchers on the effects of personality traits and crime have obtained mixed findings (Sutherland, Cressey, and Linkenbill 1992); others have found a correlation between personality traits and crime (Caspi et al. 1994).

Bartol explains that psychopaths are "skillful at pretending deep af-fection, and they may effectively mimic appropriate emotions, but true loyalty, warmth, and compassion are foreign to them" (1991, p. 63). This is clearly reminiscent of Iago. Throughout, he feigns loyalty to Othello. While he insidiously plants murderous thoughts in Othello's mind, he never has any sense of guilt about what would happen nor any remorse about the eventual death of Desdemona, nor any about killing his own wife.

SUMMARY

The theories of Lombrosianism become evident in an analysis of the character of Richard III. Through his descriptions of himself and those of others, the picture of a crooked, unsightly person is painted. The shame and anger he internalizes because nature has been unkind to him leads Richard III to act out violently. The nexus between an abnormal physic and criminality is established in Richard III.

Through Richard III, one can also make the connection between heredity and criminality. Richard was born into an outlawed family. It is therefore no surprise that Richard grows up to be a criminal himself. Although theories of heredity have been heavily criticized, some researchers continue to attach importance to them.

Iago was analyzed as a psychopath. Theories about psychopathy and the antisocial personality contend that criminal behavior originates in the personality of the offender.

8

Ecological Theory: Pompey, Froth

Robert Park and Ernest Burgess pioneered ecological theory and research in Chicago in the early 1900s. C. Shaw and H. Mckay developed ecological theory after rejecting explanations of crime causation that dealt with cultural and racial factors. Instead, they viewed the ecological conditions of the city as the reason behind criminal behavior. Their theory was geared at explaining the relationship among humans, their resources, and their social and cultural patterns. Park and Burgess, on the other hand, viewed crime as a product of a decadent "transitional neighborhood" with obvious patterns of social disorganization and "conflicting values and social systems" (Park and Burgess 1925, p. 55).

Shaw and Mckay further noted certain areas in Chicago where delinquent youths were found. Following Park and Burgess, they observed that Chicago could be divided into distinct ecological areas which formed "concentric zones" with some including more delinquents than others. The first zone from the city's center radiating outward is the factory zone, followed by the zone of transition, the workmen's zone, the residential zone, and, finally, the commuters' zone. The researchers found that the highest crime rates were found in the factory and transitional zones. They observed that, because of the competing conventional values in these areas, people are forced to choose and identify with the set of values they share. It is for this reason that different gangs exist. They also realized that, even when the ethnic composition of the inhabitants of these zones changed, crime rates remained high. Relatively lower rates were noticed in the areas away from the center of the city. Shaw describes the concept of social disorganization as follows:

> The successive changes in the composition of population, the disintegration of the alien cultures, the diffusion of divergent cultural standards, and the gradual industrialization has led to a dissolution of the neighborhood culture and organization. The continuity of conventional neighborhood traditions and institutions is broken. Thus, the effectiveness of the neighborhood as a unit of control and as a medium for the transmission of the moral standards of society is greatly diminished. The boy who grows up in this area has little access to the cultural heritages of conventional society. For the most part, the organization of his behavior takes place through his participation in the spontaneous play groups and organized gangs with which he has contact outside of the home. . . . This area is an especially favorable habitat for the development of boys' gangs and organized criminal groups. (Shaw 1951, p. 15)

Shakespeare must have noticed that certain areas of the city attract people with weakened bonds to conventional society. In those disintegrated neighborhoods, people who share delinquent behavior align themselves to delinquent groups. Shakespeare, unlike Shaw and Mckay, did not divide the city into concentric zones; however, like Shaw and Mckay, Shakespeare observed that, because of their deviant values, those living in, or frequenting neighborhoods notorious for deviance, often came into conflict with established conventional norms which advocate adherence to laws.

Measure for Measure's Pompey and Froth, a thief and a vagrant, respectively, exemplify this line of reasoning. Mistress Overdone's disorderly houses, which were located in the suburbs, were attractive sites for deviants. Besides Pompey and Froth, who get drawn to these establishments, one learns, from Pompey, about a host of others in prison who frequented the "naughty houses." Pompey comments, "I am well acquainted here [prison] as I was in our house of profession: one would think it were Mistress Overdone's own house, for here be many of her old customers" (IV.iii.1–4). That Mistress Overdone's premises is a breeding ground for deviant behavior is well stated by Elbow, the constable: "[M]y wife; who, if she had been a woman cardinally given, might have been accused in fornication, adultery, and all uncleanliness there" (II.i.91–94).

Therefore, like Shaw and Mckay, Shakespeare observed that criminality was a response to the "adverse social conditions" that exist in certain neighborhoods. When environmental conditions, for example, "neighborhood institutions" and "public opinion," are disfunctional, that is, when unlawful behavior is accepted as normal, those who live in that environment are likely to be drawn to inappropriate behavior. Situational conditions, such as economic status and cultural values, are therefore crucial factors in explaining criminal activities in disorganized neighborhoods. The absence of involvement in meaningful activities, the insufficient supervision of youths, and the presence of delinquent friends are all factors that lead to the breakdown of a neighborhood. R. Sampson's (1986) observation that the inability to enforce coherence to laws and proper values in some neighborhoods creates social disorganization validates the findings of Shaw and Mckay. The ecological theory, as explained by Shaw and Mckay, has in large part been supported by data collected in Britain by Cullen and Agnew (1999 p. 62) and S. T. Reid (1997 p. 142). The underlying point is that neighborhoods with conflicting values and weakened control systems provide attractions for deviance and criminality.

SUMMARY

Pompey and Froth are examined in light of the prevalent cultures in the play. It is evident that these villains are attracted to groups they identify with culturally. According to proponents of cultural deviance theories, because of the competing conventional values of an area, people are inclined to choose and identify with values that are akin to theirs. Therefore, the deviants, Pompey and Froth, were attracted to the location of the disorderly houses.

9

Social Learning Theories: Othello, Richard III

In this chapter, two perspectives of social learning theory, differential association and social learning theory, are applied to an analysis of Othello and Richard III, respectively.

DIFFERENTIAL ASSOCIATION: OTHELLO

Shakespeare foreshadowed E. H. Sutherland's (1947) rendition of "differential association" through his presentation of the character of Othello. Differential association is explained in nine points which revolve around four central ideas:

1. Criminal behavior is learned in interaction with other persons in a process of communication.
2. When the behavior is learned, it includes techniques of committing the crime, which are sometimes complicated, sometimes very simple, and the specific direction of motives, drives, rationalizations, and attitudes.
3. One becomes delinquent because of an excess of definitions favorable to violation of law over definitions unfavorable to violation of law.
4. Differential associations may vary in frequency, duration, priority, and intensity. (See Sutherland 1947, pp. 6–7, for a complete discussion.)

From his association with Iago, Othello learns criminal behavior. Othello learns from Iago not only the techniques of committing crime, but also the "specific direction of motives, drives, rationalizations, and attitudes" (Sutherland 1947, pp. 6–7). As he plans the murder of Desdemona, Othello contemplates poison as the method to use: "[G]et me some poison Iago, this night" (*Othello*, IV.i.246). Iago rejects killing by poison and suggests death by strangulation instead: "[D]o it not with poison; strangle her in her bed, even the bed she hath contaminated" (IV.i.250–51). Othello immediately approves of Iago's suggestion and the "specific direction of motives and rationalizations": "[G]ood, good; the justice of it pleases: very good" (IV.i.252). Since Desdemona, in Othello's thinking, has committed adultery on her matrimonial bed, it is fitting that she be killed on that same bed.

With Iago always in his company, Othello is exposed for long periods of time to Iago's deception which intensifies as Iago produces false evidences to support his lies. Iago begins contaminating Othello's mind gradually, first by casting doubts in Othello's mind, then by reinforcing those doubts, and finally by turning the doubts into reality by producing false evidence.

The following dialogue explains the point. First, Othello becomes suspicious when Iago remarks, "Ha! I like not that" (III.iii.41) after Cassio's meeting with Desdemona.

> *Othello*: What dost thou say?
>
> *Iago*: Nothing my Lord . . .
>
> *Othello*: Was not that Cassio parted from my wife?
>
> *Iago*: Cassio, my Lord! No, sure I cannot think it, that he would steal away so guilty-like, seeing you coming. (III.iii.42–48)

Second, those suspicions are reinforced when Iago warns him to beware of Venetian women because "they do let heaven see the pranks they dare not show their husband, their best conscience is not to leave undone, but keep unknown" (III.iii.259–62).

Third, Iago turns the doubts into reality by bringing to Othello's knowledge the fact that the handkerchief Othello gave Desdemona as a gift is now being used by Cassio. This proves to be the last straw; Othello now has his mind set on murdering Desdemona, and Iago leads him on. The longer Othello is in Iago's company, the more Iago's lies intensify, and the more rationalizations Othello develops to commit murder. The main elements of the learning process are detected from Othello's behavior and from his association with Iago. First, one identifies the content of what is learned—which includes the techniques for committing crimes: "specific direction of the motives, drives, rationalizations, and attitudes" (Sutherland 1947, p. 6). Second, one detects the process through which the learning is acquired—namely, prolonged association with Iago.

Differential association theory therefore suggests that once one gets to a point where one's definition favorable to law violation surpasses one's definition unfavorable to law violation, it is almost inevitable that one will violate the law. In addition, when one is able to form rationalizations for committing a crime, and with prolonged exposure to a criminal peer, it is almost obvious that one will deviate.

According to differential association, "criminal behavior is learned" (Sutherland 1947, p. 6). It can be deduced, therefore, that Sutherland discounts biological theories of crime causation. Sutherland also asserts that "the principal part of the learning of criminal behavior occurs within intimate personal groups" (1947, p. 6). The idea here seems to be that criminality can be learned mainly by association with close peers. This, according to Cullen and Agnew, suggests that movies and newspapers play an insignificant part in the etiology of criminality (1999, p. 83). Sutherland also states that "the specific direction of motives and drives is learned from definitions of the legal codes as favorable or unfavorable" (1947, p. 6). When varying interpretations are given to what the spirit and intent of the law is, people who approve of deviance are more inclined to adhere to interpretations of the law that stray from its actual meaning. Furthermore, "the process of learning criminal behavior by association with criminal and anticriminal patterns involves all of the mechanisms that are involved in any other learning" (1947, p. 7). Criminal behavior is learned in the same way we learn any other activity, including observing, imitating, listening, reading, and other methods. Finally, according to Sutherland, "although criminal behavior is an expression of general needs and values, it is not explained by those general needs and values because noncriminal behavior is an expression of the same needs and values" (1947, p. 7). This statement suggests that it is difficult to explain why people commit crimes because it is the same reason that motivates law-abiding people to look for legitimate means to meet their needs.

SOCIAL LEARNING THEORY: RICHARD III

From an in-depth study of Richard's character, it is evident that Shakespeare entertained the likelihood that Richard's behavior is a result of a direct "conditioning" and "modeling" of his father's. More explicitly, Richard learned criminality from his father.

Akers (1994) provides an explanation of crime and deviance that embraces social learning as the cause for deviant behavior.

The principal behavioral effects come from interaction in or under the influence of those groups with which one is in differential association and which control sources and patterns of reinforcement, provide normative definitions, and expose one to behavioral modes. . . .

Deviant behavior can be expected to the extent that it has been differentially reinforced over alternative behavior (conforming or other deviant behavior) and is defined as desirable or justified when the individual is in a situation discriminative for the behavior. (Akers 1997, p. 64)

Richard, as already mentioned, is born into an outlawed family. His companions are his feuding father and those assisting in a war against the king. As they conspire to arrogate the throne, Richard listens to Warwick and York (Richard's father) approve and uphold violence:

Warwick: The bloody parliament shall this be call'd, unless Plantagenet Duke of York, be king, and bashful Henry depos'd, whose cowardice hath made us by-words to our enemies.

York: Then leave me not, my lords; be resolute; I mean to take possession of my right.

Warwick: Neither the king, nor he that loves him best, the proudest he that holds up Lancaster, dares stir a wing if Warwick shake his bells. I'll plant Plantagenet, root him up who dares:—Resolve thee, Richard; claim the English crown. (*3 Henry VI*, I.i.50–62)

Richard thus learns that violence is necessary to achieve greatness and that one need not be obdurate about it. Therefore, he goes through life engaging in fierce violence whenever he deems it necessary.

Here again, Shakespeare preempts contemporary theories of crime. Richard's subsequent behavior in *Richard III* could therefore be explained by the following variables: prior exposure to deviant behavior models, association with deviant company, and parental reinforcement. Those variables that form the bedrock of Akers' theory—"differential association, differential re-inforcement, imitation, and definitions, singly and in combination" (Akers 1997, p. 75)—are evidenced in Richard's behavior. According to Akers, differential association refers to the process whereby a person interacts with lawbreakers and adopts their values and mores. Differential reinforcement refers to approvals (tacit or implicit) and rewards that accompany criminal behavior. Imitation refers to those acts of deviance that a person emulates from his associates through observation. Definitions relate to the criminal's own assessment which he or she attaches to behavior (see Akers 1997, pp. 62–69).

Akers explains the social learning theory: "Social learning theory offers an explanation of crime and deviance which embraces variables that operate both to motivate and control criminal behavior, both to promote and undermine conformity" (1997, p. 63). Put simply, criminal behavior is learned when one is exposed to indoctrinations of lawbreaking by other criminals.

SUMMARY

This chapter deals with two types of social learning theory. The first type examines Othello's character, and through interpretations of his behavior, a connection is made with Sutherland's differential association. From the story lines, the point is made that criminal behavior and techniques of carrying out criminal enterprises are learned through prolonged exposure to peers with criminal tendencies.

Those with whom Richard III associates are criminals who regard lawlessness as a virtue. It is with these people (including Richard's own father) that Richard interacts and thereby learns no mode of behavior other than aggression. Akers' learning theory addresses the influence of deviant and criminal acquaintances on a person. Criminal tendencies, he postulates, are passed on to a person through interaction and reinforcement.

10
Social Control and Bond Theories: Lady Macbeth, Othello, Richard III

SOCIAL CONTROL THEORY: TECHNIQUES OF NEUTRALIZATION AND DRIFT: LADY MACBETH, OTHELLO

In his observations of human behavior, Shakespeare must have noticed that, although people respect conventional values much of the time, they sometimes learn or develop techniques that enable them to counteract the effectiveness of these values and laws and "drift" toward illegitimate behavior. The characters of Lady Macbeth in *Macbeth* and Othello in *Othello* illustrate this perspective.

In the 1950s G. Sykes and D. Matza developed a similar line of thought which they called neutralization/drift theory. Through the use of "techniques of neutralization," people can temporarily put conventional values in abeyance and drift into nonconformity or "subterranean" behaviors. They cite five techniques of neutralization (1957, pp. 664–690): (1) *Denial of responsibility*. People applying this technique usually disclaim responsibility and instead blame their behavior on others. Batterers and abusers use this technique much of the time. They blame their behavior on the fact that they were themselves victims of abuse at an early age. (2) *Denial of injury*. One denies the wrongfulness of one's action by arguing that no one was really hurt or by minimizing the extent of the victim's injury. (3) *Denial of victim*. Here, one justifies one's action by asserting that the victim brought it upon himself or herself: the offender's act was justified. (4) *Condemnation of the condemners*. The offender passes on blame to others, for example, those who denounce the offender's actions. According to Cullen and Agnew, the offender may claim that those who condemn him or her are "hypocrites, deviants in disguise, or impelled by personal spite" (1999, pp. 89–90). (5) *Appeal to higher loyalties.* The lawbreaker acts in compliance with the demands of his or her associates: one's loyalty to another or to a group is greater than to the law.

The characters of Lady Macbeth and Othello can be used to explain these neutralizing techniques. Prior to the murder of Duncan, the Macbeths were law-abiding citizens, and as a general in the king's army, Macbeth fought bravely on behalf of the king. Along come the witches with their prophesy of greatness. The Macbeths embrace it and use it as a neutralizing factor to indulge in treason. Lady Macbeth reads the missive from Macbeth:

> these weird sisters saluted me, and referred me to the coming on of time, with hail, king that shalt be! This have I thought good to deliver thee, my dearest partner of greatness; that thou mightst not lose the dues of rejoicing, by being ignorant of what greatness is promised thee. Lay it to thy heart, and farewell. (I.v.9–15)

Lady Macbeth now has a pretext, a rationalization, to commit a crime: "Glamis thou art, and Cawdor," she says, "and shalt be what thou art promis'd" (I.v.16–17). Lady Macbeth takes this promise seriously and suspends any further loyalty toward the king because only with their kingly allegiance withdrawn can she and her husband free themselves to commit murder. She constantly reminds herself of the fact that the idea of becoming king is not of human origin but something willed by supernatural powers: "[F]ate and metaphysical aid doth seem to have thee crown'd withal" (I.v.35–36). She therefore sees their act as a fulfillment of some wish expected by some power other than theirs. That power, in Shakespeare's mind, is obviously satanic. They thus rationalize their crime as an appeal to higher loyalties. With that conviction, she deviates from conventional behavior.

Othello's character also illuminates Shakespeare's views on neutralizing techniques. Prior to going astray, Othello is a loving husband and a law-abiding person. After Iago deceives him into believing that Desdemona is unfaithful to him, Othello plans murder. As suggested by the neutralizing technique that Sykes and Matza refer to as a "denial of victim," Othello insulates himself from guilt by asserting, that his crime is a result of a deserved retaliation: "Think on thy sins. . . . Ay, and for that thou diest" (V.ii.52, 54). Desdemona supposedly has committed adultery; for that, she must die. Othello employs another neutralizing technique—appealing to higher loyalties. The killing of Desdemona is to save more men from betrayal: "[Y]et she must die, else she'll betray more men" (V.ii.6). These techniques are merely rationalizations or excuses for rejecting the values of conventional norms.

In essence, Lady Macbeth and Othello contend that their crimes are guiltless because there are overriding mitigating circumstances which negate any wrongdoing on their part. In explaining neutralization/drift theory, Vold and Bernard maintain that lawbreakers do not disapprove of conventional moral values but "neutralize them in a wide variety of circumstances so that they are able to commit delinquent actions and still consider themselves guiltless" (1986, p. 240). People drift in to law-breaking by convincing themselves that their act is intended to serve some better end. These techniques, which are merely defense mechanisms, in essence liberate a person from the restrictions of the law and conventional morality.

SOCIAL BOND THEORY: RICHARD III

Contemporary control/bond theory argues that the social bond a person maintains with society in a large sense determines a person's conformity to social norms and values. Without social bonds or with weakened social bonds, and in the absence of sensitivity to and interest in others, a person is more likely to resort to criminality.

T. Hirschi (1969) postulates four variables of the social bond: *attachment, commitment, involvement,* and *belief.* His social bond theory examines the reasons why some people do not commit crimes. Because this theory hinges on two concepts, a person's *bond* to *society,* it is inevitable that, at different points in time, the theory has been employed to explain deviant or criminal behavior (Cullen and Agnew 1999, p. 168).

Although Shakespeare did not espouse social bond theory in the late fifteenth and sixteenth centuries as it is known today, when one reads his writings carefully and understands the character of Richard III, one is able to identify many of the elements present in the bond or control theory. Tracing Richard's life from *2 Henry VI* enables one to see that the social controls in Richard's life were weak, and he was therefore "free" to commit crime.

One of the controls Shakespeare writes a great deal about is attachment to significant others. Attachment, as Hirschi explains, refers to a person's "sensitivity" to others. When people are concerned about how others view them, and they care about others' expectations, they are less likely to offend. Hirschi stresses that attachment to parents and parental supervision are helpful in controlling deviance; the corollary is that, if those significant others do not show their children affection, the children do not care what they do. Therefore, because there is no expectation from the children, they have no "stake in conformity." Shakespeare insinuates in his writings that because Richard lacks love and affection from those close to him, he too is incapable of giving love. Richard makes it clear that he has no concept of love: "[T]his word love, which greybirds call divine, be resident in men like one another, and not in me; I am myself alone" (3 Henry VI, V.vi.98–101).

Love and affection from significant others such as parents, siblings, friends, and teachers in a large measure help people conform to the laws of society. Therefore, the more insensitive those significant others are, the more likely people are to deviate from abiding by those values and laws they share. From the day he is born, Richard is "less than a mother's hope . . . an indigest deformed lump" (V.vi.60, 62). No one is excited about his birth. As he is told, even the midwife who assists in his delivery wondered together with the other women, "Oh Jesus bless us, he is born with teeth!" (V.vi.92). No one ever cared about Richard. The only appreciation Richard gets comes from his father after Richard displays valor at the battle of St. Albans: "Richard hath best deserv'd of all my sons" (I.i.17). His mother, who naturally ought to provide the most affection for Richard, finds his birth a severe burden: "[T]hou cam'st on earth to make the earth my hell. A grievous burden was thy birth to me. . . . What comfortable hour canst thou name that ever grac'd me in thy company?" (Richard III, IV.iv.300, 309–310). From birth, the ties that bind Richard to society are weak. He cares less what he does because no one cares about him or, therefore, the things he does. The feeling that no one cares, control theorists state, stay with a person throughout that person's life.

Thus, a person whose bond to society is weak is exposed to crimogenic behavior at any age. This indeed is Richard's fate. As his mother tells him, "Tetchy and wayward was thy infancy; thy school days frightful, desperate, wild, and furious; thy prime of manhood daring, bold, and venturous (IV.iv.302–5). So, at no stage of his life did Richard know discipline.

Besides having weak ties to his mother, Richard's ties to his siblings are weak: "I have no brother, I am like no brother" (3 Henry VI, V.vi.97). Richard would like to spend time in the company of ladies, but because he is badly deformed, he cannot "prove a lover." Since he is cheated by nature and can find no one to love him, he is "determined to prove a villain" (Richard III, I.i.33). Richard is a loner; the friends he has are merely allies in war; and, as stated, he does not hesitate to kill anyone who does not comply to his wishes.

Another control of Hirschi's theory is commitment. According to the theory, a person with commitments, that is, who has invested time, energy, or money, into any venture, will be less inclined to engage in any activity that might destroy his or her reputation. The logical proposition is that a person who has nothing to lose might more easily engage in deviant behavior. An examination of Richard's character shows that, although he was Duke of Gloster and later king, all he knew in life was violence. He earned all of his titles through violence and chicanery.

Hirschi explains that involvement in conventional activities, such as studying, and participation in positive activities, such as a job, diminish a person's likelihood to be involved in deviant activities. It is evident that Richard was not a serious student, for as his mother explains, his school days were "frightful, desperate, wild, and furious." Shakespeare must have observed that the emotional instability Richard experienced, coupled with the fact that he had nothing meaningful to preoccupy him, set him up for a life of destruction.

Control theory suggests that people who accept conventional values and laws and who respect the rights of others are less likely to break laws or infringe on the rights of others. Conversely, those who have little or no respect for the law and the rights of others are more likely to breach those laws and to violate the rights of others. According to Hirschi "There is variation in the extent to which people believe they should obey the rules of society, and, furthermore, that the less a person believes he should obey the rules, the more likely he is to violate them" (1969, p. 26).

Shakespeare must have viewed Richard in this light. Richard had no respect for the law or for the rights of others. As he stabs King Henry, Richard declares, "I that have neither pity, love, nor fear" (3 *Henry VI*, V.vi.68). It is easy for him to destroy as he pleases with no remorse and with no fear of reprisals.

Control theory thus explains criminality through the weakening of a person's bonds to society. If a person has close ties to significant others, is preoccupied with conventional activities, and respects the laws of society, he or she is less likely to deviate. The likelihood to conform is thus facilitated by "the amount of time the child spends with parents, the intimacy of communication between parents and child and the affectional identification between parent and child" (Hirschi 1969, p. 53; see also Adler, Mueller, and Laufer 1998, p. 151). In addition, persons who are involved in and committed to positive activities and who have faith in laws are less likely to deviate.

SUMMARY

After examining the characters of Lady Macbeth and Othello, the realization is made that sometimes people who otherwise would not commit crimes stray away from conformity when they can rationalize their behavior. Sykes and Matza refer to this reasoning as the technique of neutralization and drift.

In the second section of Chapter 10, Richard III is discussed in light of his attachments to significant others. Richard, as we learn, has no concept of love; he feels alone and so it is irrelevant to him what others think of what he does. Hirschi's bonding theory states that when one's bond to significant others is weakened, or when one is not involved in or committed to worthwhile activities, one is "free" to resort to deviance or criminality.

11
Normalcy of Crime and Strain/Anomie Theories

NORMALITY OF CRIME: IAGO, ANGELO, CLAUDIO

It seems clear as one reads Shakespearean plays that the Bard regarded crime as a common and normal occurrence in society. When Angelo, in *Measure for Measure*, eloquently asserts, "We are all frail . . . since I suppose we are made to be no stronger than faults may shake our frames" (II.iv.140, 155–56), he was merely philosophizing on the normality of crime. Because of this frailty in man, one can understand why Claudio indulges in premarital sexual activities with his fiancée, an act prohibited by Viennese statute. In like manner, because of frailty, Angelo, the deputy entrusted to cleanse Vienna of crime, fornicates, an offense for which he has sentenced Claudio to die.

Through these characters Shakespeare is making the point that although we generally want to be law abiding, because of human nature we occasionally deviate from the norms. Furthermore, Shakespeare seems to be making the point that it is sometimes necessary for us to deviate because it is only through breaking the rules that we learn more about ourselves and how we can make more realistic changes in society. Angelo does not know himself; indeed, he has no inkling that he is capable of contravening the law. When he confidently proclaims, "When I, that censure him [Claudio], do so offend, let mine own judgment pattern out my death, and nothing come in partial" (II.i.29–31), little does he know how his words will come to haunt him.

Angelo's violation of the law against lechery is a wake-up call for the

Viennese lawmakers because they now realize that the penalty for fornication is too strict. Shakespeare's point is that man can never live up to laws legalistically: it takes grace; that is how men should treat each other. Instead of implementing the death penalty for fornication, other lesser penalties are imposed.

Shakespeare must also have created Iago's character to caution us to beware of our actions and our dealings with others, whom we trust and the extent to which we trust others. Othello, lamenting, reminds us, "[T]hen must you speak of one that lov'd not wisely, but too well; of one not easily jealous, but, being wrought, of one whose hand . . . threw a pearl away" (V.ii.450–55). Shakespeare's portrayal of Iago is a reminder to us that there are certain people in society who do not like to see others happy, and by subtle or obvious means they try to stifle the happiness of others.

Shakespeare also seems to suggest that in order to restate the integrity of a society, certain acts have to be considered criminal. It is through the fear of punishment that others may be deterred. When sexual intercourse between unmarried people is punishable by death in Vienna, it is intended to suppress widespread lechery.

Centuries later, Emile Durkheim, the first sociological pioneer to consider crime, had a similar perspective. Durkheim posited that crime is a "normal and necessary social behavior" and that this "normalcy" of crime is a result of the differences of people in a society. Since we are different from one another and never receive identical inputs, we are bound to behave differently. It follows that some people will deviate from conventional values to meet their needs.

Durkheim also discussed the necessity of crime. R. Martin, R. Mutchnick, and T. Austin (1990) have analyzed Durkheim's ideas. First, social change is sometimes brought about because someone breaks the norms. At the time when the norm is breached, it is difficult to ascertain whether the criminal act will lead to progress. Second, crime is functional because it provides cues that change is necessary. Lawmakers can then provide measures to circumvent the antisocial behavior. Third, crime may be important for the purposes of general deterrence. Fourth, crime brings unity.

When writing about the normality of crime in society, Durkheim argued that because the causes of anomic situations vary, normlessness could occur in periods of economic decline, as well as in times of prosperity. In times of depression, the stress causes lawlessness; in times of prosperity, lawlessness is caused by an increase in people's expectations, or "appetites."

At every moment in history there is a deem perception, in the moral consciousness of societies, of the respective value of different social services, the relative reward due each, and the consequent degree of comfort appropriate on the average to workers in each occupation. . . . Under this pressure, each in his sphere vaguely realizes the extreme limit set to his ambitions and aspires to nothing beyond. . . . Thus, an end and goal are set to the passions. (Durkheim 1951, pp. 246–53)

In explaining Durkheim's perspective, Reid remarks:

For a society to be flexible enough to permit positive deviation, it must permit negative deviation as well. If no deviation is permitted, societies become stagnant. Crime helps prepare society for such changes. (1997, p. 143)

Therefore, crime is a normal response in every society, and it indicates a need for social change.

STRAIN/ANOMIE THEORY: FALSTAFF, POMPEY, FROTH

When Shakespeare created the characters of Falstaff, Pompey, and Froth, he understood the social patterns about which Durkheim and R. K. Merton wrote extensively centuries later. Durkheim, writing in the nineteenth century in France, introduced the concept of anomie (normlessness) in the *Division of Labor in Society* (1893) and later expounded on it in *Suicide* (1897). According to Durkheim, the occurrence of crime in society is an indication of human differences. Since people are different, we employ different methods and exhibit different behavioral traits to meet our needs. Therefore, it is inevitable that some people will resort to deviant ways to meet certain needs. Normlessness, according to Durkheim, is a breakdown of the rules of society.

In 1938 Merton used Durkheim's insights to explain deviance in the United States. Merton analyzed social norms in two ways: (1) societal goals, for example, wealth, and (2) the acceptable means for achieving those goals. Due to the structure of society, according to Merton, emphasis is placed on certain goals (e.g., the acquisition of wealth), but at the same time the legitimate procedures for attaining these ends are unevenly distributed. Some people are able to attain this goal through institutionally prescribed ways; others are frustrated and "strained" because of their inability to meet their ends through conventional ways. The path they thereafter resort to may be deviant.

Merton states five modes of adaptation: (1) conformity, (2) innovation, (3) ritualism, (4) retreatism, (5) rebellion. *Conformity* is the route most people take. This involves respect for institutionally prescribed modes of attaining the goals of society. By *innovation* people accept the goals but

94

Criminological Theory and Behavior

resort to nonapproved means to meet their needs. This is the most deviant mode of adaptation. In *ritualism*, emphasis is not placed on the goals; however, the prescribed means are rigidly adhered to. *Retreatism* involves rejection of both the goals and the means of society. People in this category give up on themselves and typically become vagrants, drunkards, tramps, and drug addicts. In *rebellion*, conventional goals and means are substituted for new goals and means.

Falstaff, Pompey, and some of the characters Pompey meets in prison exemplify how deviance is created as a result of the structuring of society. Shakespeare is suggesting through these characters that if the means of achieving goals is limited to only some, it becomes inevitable that some members of the deprived segment will adapt to deviant ways to attain that goal. In *1 Henry IV*, Falstaff and others learn that rich travelers and traders with "fat purses" are leaving a hotel for their various destinations, and they immediately contrive a plan to rob the travelers. Falstaff, as we know, is a drunkard with no clear source of income. He contemplates theft at all times. He is in debt and can hardly pay for basic necessities, such as food, as we learn from the hostess of the tavern: "You owe money here, Sir John, for your diet and by drinkings, and money lent you, four-and-twenty pound" (III.iii.82–84). Shakespeare uses Falstaff to make the point that when people want vertical mobility and are incapable of obtaining it through societally precribed ways, the resulting conflict forces them to apply innovative solutions. Falstaff is made head of an infantry and he is given a budget. It is not surprising that Falstaff, who is constantly in debt, keeps for his personal use the funds allocated for the soldiers.

Pompey, a petty employee of Mistress Overdone, also steals and is sentenced to prison where he meets a host of members of the lower class who are former clients of Mistress Overdone. Many of them are incarcerated for property crimes as we learn from Pompey:

> First, here's young Master Rush; he's in for a commodity of brown paper and old ginger, ninescore and seventeen pounds; . . . then is there here one Master Caper, at the suit of Master Threepile . . . for some four suits of peach-coloured satin. . . . Then have we here young Dizy, and young Master Deepvow, and Master Copperspur and Master Starvelackey. (*Measure for Measure*, IV.iii.4–16)

The vagrant Froth neatly fits Merton's retreatist category. Froth commits no crime and is not vicious. He is an idler, with no discernible purpose in life. He has clearly accepted his fate as a dropout, rejecting both society's goals and means.

The central idea behind the creation of these characters is that Shakespeare wants us to know that "anomic situations" develop in societies which cannot or do not provide defined opportunities to guide behavior and aspirations. When a society stresses success but fails to provide adequate means of attaining it, it becomes inevitable that the resulting pressure will generate crime and other retreatist behavior such as drug use, drunkeness, and vagrancy. Strain theory thus maintains that certain forces in the social structure propel people who are deprived of meeting their needs through legitimate ways to commit crimes (Mannheim 1967, p. 504).

SUMMARY

Angelo, Claudio, and Iago become lawbreakers by using deviant means to satisfy their various urges. Through these characters, Shakespeare instructs us that we may not know ourselves as well as we think we do. Sometimes it is only by deviating and contravening the laws of society that we learn more about ourselves and how we can make meaningful changes. Lawmakers are also more inclined to promulgate laws that emphasize conformity to legitimate norms when lawlessness is prevalent.

According to Durkheim, crime is an obvious and necessary response to various human needs. The fact that each person is endowed with a unique trait makes it inevitable that responses to a stimulus will differ. It follows that people will employ different methods to meet their needs.

Falstaff, Pompey, and Froth exemplify the problems inherent in a society that does not provide equal opportunities for all to attain upward mobility. When some segments of society are lacking in legitimate means to satisfy their needs, they are likely to adopt different means, including preying on others to fulfill those needs.

Merton's strain theory espouses different modes of adaptation employed by those "strained" due to their inability to attain the goals of society. Some of these modes, for example innovation and rebellion, stray from conventional norms.

12

Social Reaction/Labeling Theory: Shylock

Labeling theorists argue that we can understand criminal and deviant behavior only in the context of the reaction of others to it, and also through the ways in which law officials define and react to the behavior. These theorists contend that criminals are not inherently evil people committing illegal acts; rather, they are people who have had the status of "criminal" imposed on them by both society and the criminal justice system. Therefore, it is the reaction of society to a person's behavior that determines how that person views himself or herself thereafter.

> *Social groups create deviance by making the rules whose infraction constitutes deviance,* and by applying those rules to particular people and labeling them as outsiders. From this point of view, deviance is not a quality of the act the person commits, but rather a consequence of the application by others of the rules and sanctions to an 'offender.' The deviant is one to whom that label has successfully been applied; deviant behavior is behavior that people so label. (Becker 1963, p. 9; emphasis in original)

F. Tannenbaum, writing about the "dramatization of evil" in *Crime and the Community*, preceded E. Lemert and H. Becker in espousing views on social reaction theory.

> The process of making the criminal, therefore, is a process of tagging, defining, identifying, segregating, describing, emphasizing,

making conscious and self-conscious; it becomes a way of stimu-
lating, suggesting, emphasizing, and evoking the very traits that
are complained of. (1938, p. 20)

Vold and Bernard decipher labeling theory in four points: (1) the definition of crime, (2) the origins of criminal behaviors and the effect that
defining an individual as a criminal has on that individual's behavior,
(3) the processes by which agents of the criminal justice system arrive at
official definitions of specific people and events as criminal, (4) the processes by which general categories of behavior are defined as crimes in
the criminal law (1986, p. 250).

These same ideas are evident in Shakespeare's *The Merchant of Venice.*
Shakespeare's ideas will be explained in the context of Vold and Bernard's four theoretical arguments. (1) *The definition of crime*: According
to Vold and Bernard, labeling theorists employ the words "deviance"
and "social reaction" to explain how people and certain acts come to be
known as criminal and crime, respectively. The behavior is criminal because society and the law determine that. Shylock epitomizes a deviant
who comes to be seen that way because one group of people view him
so. Shylock's suit against Antonio is a suit to recover a debt. However,
midway through the trial, Shylock suddenly becomes the defendant. Portia, the trial lawyer, finds in Shylock's gestures, words, and demeanor
an intent to commit grievous bodily harm. Thereafter, Shylock is at the
mercy of the court charged with a felony:

> Tarry, Jew; the law hath yet another hold on you. . . . It appears by
> manifest proceeding, that indirectly, and directly too, thou hast
> contriv'd against the very life of the defendant, and thou has in-
> curr'd the danger [execution] formerly by me rehears'd. (IV.i.327–
> 42)

Shylock's plight is a result of a "reactive definition of crime" since
labeling theorists posit that "crime is defined solely by the reactions of
other people to it" (Vold and Bernard 1986, p. 251). Labeling theorists
argue that "acts are not intrinsically bad"; they are made bad by criminal
law. It follows that the commission of a deviant act is not in itself what
makes one a deviant or a criminal. Those empowered to enforce the law
define which act becomes criminal. Shylock thought he was only trying
to enforce the terms of the contract. He was surprised he was charged
with a crime.

(2) *Origins of criminal behavior and the effect of the label*: Labeling theorists contend that people who commit crimes are often likely to think of
themselves as criminals even when they do not commit crimes; that is,
they develop a self-image of a criminal. This view, which stems from

symbolic interactionism, holds that "the mind and the self are not innate but are products of the social environment" (Vold and Bernard 1986, p. 252). Hence, our "self-concepts" are determined by people's reactions to our various roles. As Vold and Bernard explain, when we make certain claims of ourselves we must, in order to have the claim stick, "validate it by meeting the cultural criteria of the role" (1986, p. 252). When one is labeled a "thief" for instance, there is a possibility that a person will react to that label. Lemert (1951) calls this "secondary deviance."

Throughout *The Merchant of Venice*, Shylock is referred to as a "Jew" more often in a derogatory manner than in reference to his race. The insinuation is that he is wicked or unkind: "As seek to soften that,— than which what's harder?—His Jewish heart" (IV.i.79–80); "Hie thee, gentle Jew; This Hebrew will turn Christian: he grows kind" (I.iii.179–80); "Thou shalt have nothing but the forfeiture to be so taken at thy peril, Jew" (IV.i.333); "currish Jew"; "harsh Jew." Antonio, whose flesh Shylock seeks to cut, advises Bassanio to quit requesting mercy from Shylock because, as Antonio states, it is a needless effort—Shylock will not relent:

> I pray you, think you question with the Jew:
> You may as well go stand upon the beach
> And bid the main-flood bait his usual height;
> You may as well use question with the wolf
> You may as well forbid the mountain pines
> To wag their high tops, and to make no noise,
> When they are fretted with the gusts of heaven;
> You may as well do anything most hard
> As seek to soften that,—than which what's harder?
> His Jewish heart.—Therefore, I do beseech you,
> Make no more offers, use no further means,
> But, withall brief and plain conveniency,
> Let me have judgment and the Jew his will. (IV.i.79–93)

Following these poor perceptions of himself, Shylock remains heartless as was expected of him, a Jew. As labelist theorists would say, he reacts to the perception of him. Until the end, Shylock remains the "cruel devil." He declares, "Proceed to judgment: by my soul I swear there is no power in the tongue of man to alter me.—I stay here on my bond (IV.i.266–68).

(3) *How the criminal justice system defines certain behavior as criminal*: In explaining how the criminal justice system comes to refer to certain acts as crimes, Vold and Bernard explain that agents of the law give meaning to a situation; that is, they "define" it as a crime, and then they act on that meaning (1986, p. 257). In addition, as Vold and Bernard explain,

other nonlegal factors contribute in the decision to call an act a crime: "interaction with the offender, the interaction with the complainant, the organizational structure, policy of the agency, and the demands of the particular job" (1986, p. 257). These factors contribute to the "enforcement of criminal laws."

In interacting with the offender, the police decision to file charges is based on the officer's impression of the character of the offender instead of the offense (1986, pp. 257–58). In a court of justice in Venice, the Duke, Portia, Bassanio, and Gratiano assess Shylock's character. The Duke and Portia, who are judge and prosecutor respectively, listen to Shylock, watch his temperament, and decide whether to define his action a crime. In reaching a decision to charge Shylock with a crime, a number of "cues" are considered: Shylock's unwillingness to be merciful, his unwillingness to take money thrice the amount owed him in lieu of Antonio's flesh, his race, and his demeanor. In a study cited by Vold and Bernard, demeanor is a major factor in between 50 and 60 percent of the decisions police make to file charges (p. 258). Shylock's demeanor seems to have played a huge part in the outcome of his lawsuit.

The Duke, in an out-of-court session, tries to no avail to persuade Shylock to drop his suit against Antonio. The Duke is thus left with a very poor impression of Shylock which he makes known to Antonio, "I am sorry for thee; thou art come to answer a stony adversary, an inhuman wretch uncapable of pity, void and empty from any dram of mercy" (IV.i.3–6). Bassanio, one of the witnesses, remarks about Shylock, "[T]herefore thou unfeeling man, to excuse the current of the cruelty" (IV.i.63–64). Gratiano, another witness, exclaims to Shylock, "[I]nexorable dog! . . . thou almost mak'st me waver in my faith, to hold opinion . . . that souls of animals infuse themselves into the trunks of men: thy currish spirit" (IV.i.149, 151, 153–54). Finally, Portia's solemn plea in the celebrated "quality of mercy" speech falls on deaf ears. The court is ready to give Shylock "justice more than [he] desir'st" (IV.i.355). This reaction of the court fits Vold and Bernard's explanation: when a suspect's demeanor is hostile to law enforcement officers, the officers "feel maligned and they soon become defensively cynical and aggressively moralistic" (p. 258).

(4) *Process by which categories of behavior are defined as criminal in law*: Labeling theorists argue that society "creates" crime by its laws. In trying to minimize bad behavior, criminal law defines certain behavior as criminal thus creating a class of people with that tag. These laws, as Vold contends, are brought about through the influences of groups of people with more power than other groups. The laws are intended to maintain the interests and values of the powerful group.

In *The Merchant of Venice*, Shylock's gestures are immediately construed as criminal because the laws of Venice protect its citizens against aliens. Shylock, who is a Jew and thus an alien, is automatically considered a threat to Antonio, a Venetian, and thus is charged with a felony:

> Tarry, Jew;
> The law hath yet another hold of you.
> It is enacted in the laws of Venice,—
> If it be prov'd against an alien,
> That by direct or indirect attempts
> He seek the life of any citizen,
> The party 'gainst the which he doth contrive
> Shall seize one half his goods; the other half
> Comes to the privy coffer of the state;
> And the offender's life lies in the mercy
> Of the Duke only, 'gainst all other voice. (IV.i.389–95)

Social reaction or labeling theory thus maintains that the reaction of other people and the consequences of those reactions create crime and deviance. According to F. Adler, G. Mueller, and W. Laufer, "Those in power create the laws, decide who will be the rule breakers and the process that defines or labels certain persons as criminals" (1995, p. 180). In Shylock's case, it is decided that aliens will be the lawbreakers. Because he is a Jew, an alien, Shylock is automatically a criminal. Labeling theorists also argue that when society labels a person a criminal, in time that person sees himself or herself as a criminal and thus gears his or her behavior to fit that label. As Tannenbaum contends, an accused's self-image changes from the time of arrest. Some stigma attaches to him thereafter and "the person becomes the thing he is described as being" (1938, p. 20).

In recent times, labeling theory has been discredited on the grounds that empirically its propositions have not been supported. However, R. Triplett and R. Jarjoura (1994) concede that the theory is still useful in sparking research and in influencing public policy.

SUMMARY

Throughout *The Merchant of Venice*, Shylock is referred to as the Jew more so as a derogation than as a reference to his race. Since it was the perception at the time that Jews were unkind, Shylock was not expected to show mercy to Antonio. He indeed acted in keeping with the perception of him.

In interpreting how behavior comes to be labeled criminal, labeling theorists contend that agents of the law give that meaning to it. When Shylock is intransigent and demands to have a pound of flesh from Antonio's chest in compliance with the bond, his behavior is construed as criminal by Portia and by the Duke.

13
Conflict Theory: Shylock

The Merchant of Venice illustrates Shakespeare's ability to shift from a classicalist to a positivist and, finally, to a conflict orientation. Shakespeare probably considered economic conditions (wealth) a source of evil in society.

According to W. Bonger, an early advocate of Marxist theory, the "profit motive found in capitalist society, induces egoistic tendencies," encourages greed and selfishness, and fails to promote "social instincts" which would otherwise prevent "egoistic thoughts from leading to egoistic acts" (quoted in Akers 1994, p. 164). As a consequence of the capitalist economic system, humans have "become very egoistic, and hence more capable of crime than if the environment had developed the germs of altruism" (Bonger quoted in Akers 1994, p. 164).

Richard Quinney, an advocate of conflict theory, views crimes committed by all classes of society as a consequence of the capitalist system. When Shylock signs the infamous bond with Antonio, he does not know that his action will be considered criminal. The point is implied here that, since the law constitutes the values of lawmakers, it is likely that the law will criminalize the actions of anyone out of this power structure. In explaining conflict in society, Quinney (1980) addresses the point that "agents of law" create crime by enacting laws that define certain behavior as criminal.

Falstaff and Pompey prey on others because they need things money can be used to buy. Shylock attempts to commit bodily harm in order to protect his monetary interest. This view seems to emanate from the idea that crime is a by-product of capitalism.

Shakespeare had foreseen the evils of an economic system in which the means of production, distribution, and ownership are not evenly distributed, even before the capitalist revolution. Those with limited opportunities in the system look for equity by becoming parasites; those with wealth seek to solidify their position in whatever means possible. While Shakespeare realizes that those with economic power are more inclined to influence the legal system, he also recognizes that other social factors—for instance, one's race and religion—could make it impossible for a uniform application of the law. So, while Shylock had the economic advantage on his side, his defenseless social position as a Jew worked against him. The system does not only relinquish ownership of his property, it compels him to change his religious inclination to Christianity based on Antonio's suggestion:

> So please my lord the Duke, and all the court
> To quit the fine for one half of his goods;
> I am content, so he will let me have
> The other half in use, to render it,
> Upon his death, unto the gentleman
> That lately stole his daughter:
> Two things provided more,—that for this favour,
> He presently become a Christian;
> The other, that he do record a gift,
> Here in the court, of all he dies possess'd
> Unto his son Lorenzo and his daughter. (IV.i.426–437)

When Shylock drew the bond to cut a pound of flesh from Antonio's chest, he was not acting out of financial desperation. He drew such an unconscionable contract in part out of greed and in part out of revenge: "He [Antonio] lends out money gratis, and brings down the rate of usuance here with us in Venice. If I can catch him once upon the hip, I will feed fat the ancient grudge I bear him" (I.iii.46–49). Shakespeare, through this speech, exposes the evils of greed in a society that subscribes to private ownership of wealth. As Bonger (1916) explains, the capitalist economic system promotes greediness and selfishness and encourages people to look out for themselves without paying any regard for others. The lack of concern for the welfare of the entire society, as Bonger suggests, explains crime in capitalist societies (see Vold and Bernard 1986, p. 303). R. Quinney does not consider crime a product of "individual pathology"—instead, he sees it as "a judgement made by some about the actions and characteristics of others" (1970, p. 16).

Based on Shylock's demeanor, actions, and utterances, he was made a defendant in a lawsuit in which he was initially a plaintiff. It follows that Shakespeare had indeed perceived Quinney's assertion that crime is a product of the perception of those in power. Those in power define behavior, institute rules about how people should conduct themselves, and enforce conformity through social control.

SUMMARY

Shylock's behavior and speech are instrumental in making him a defendant in a lawsuit in which he initially was the plaintiff. The trial scene of *The Merchant of Venice* reveals how easily one can become a criminal based upon the decisions of those in power. Shylock had no idea that his determination to have the terms of his contract with Antonio enforced would be construed as criminal by the authorities of the court. Shakespeare had thus preempted conflict theorists like Quinney who maintain that crime is the product of the perceptions of those in control of the power structure.

14
Integrated Theories

Since the emergence of criminology as a discipline, criminologists have sought to explain why people commit crimes. Several theories have been proferred, but, in the vast majority of cases, none seems to provide a complete explanation of the behavior. The trend in recent times has been to integrate theories in order to provide a more comprehensive understanding of criminal behavior. Theory integration can be defined as follows:

> A perspective that seeks to expand and synthesize earlier positions into a modern analytical device with great explanatory and predictive power. A blend of seemingly independent concepts into coherent explanations of criminality. (Champion 1997, p. 65)

Efforts in theory integration have often entailed the combination of two or more related theories, or the expansion of an existing theory by introducing new variables which, in some instances, are taken from other theories (see, for example, strain theory and the variations of the theory in Merton 1938; and Cloward and Ohlin 1960). Although there has been a debate as to the viability of theory integration and theory competition (see Hirschi 1979; Gottfredson and Hirschi 1990; Elliott 1985), the move toward integration and competition of theories has not been stifled. Theory competition, as defined by Akers, is "the logical, conceptual, or empirical comparisons of two or more theories to determine which offers the better or best explanation of crime" (1997, p. 205). Akers also outlines examples of theories that have been integrated (p. 208).

T. P. Thornberry (1987) combines social control and social learning theories to derive what he refers to as an "interactional theory of delinquency." Thornberry explains how the processes involved in both theories have a mutual effect on each other and how, over time, the variables may diminish in their influence on criminality. This explains why some people refrain from criminal activities and why some persist in a life of crime.

T. E. Moffitt (1997) combines biological and sociological variables to explain why some criminals may continue in a lifetime of criminality and why offending behavior may cease in some individuals at adolescence. Her "adolescent-limited and life course-persistent offending" theory and Thornberry's "interactional theory of delinquency" are discussed in light of the character Richard III.

PATHWAYS IN THE LIFE COURSE TO CRIME: RICHARD III

The factors that lead people to crime and deviance are complex. Why some people desist from criminal activities and why others persist in a life of crime have not so far been adequately explained by a single theory. Some characters discussed in this book appear to be first-time offenders (Othello); others (e.g., Froth) refrain from deviance after being reprimanded by the constable. Still others (Iago and Richard III) appear to be aroused by their criminal activities. Their involvement in crime did not only span a prolonged period of time, but more important, their criminal activities were frequent and grave.

In espousing her perspective on deviance and crime, Moffitt (1997) classifies two types of antisocial personalities. One category comprises a large number of people whose involvement in crime or deviance subsides after adolescence; the other category, a small proportion of people, comprises those who engage in frequent criminal or deviant behavior for much of their lives. Moffitt refers to the two categories as "adolescent-limited" offenders and "life course-persistent" offenders, respectively.

Moffitt maintains that both biological and social factors are instrumental to the onset of criminality. She argues that certain biological traits that prompt people to deviance may be triggered by social factors that are not conducive to a stable and sociable lifestyle. While social factors may feed the biological traits, a reciprocal effect may be observed. That is, biological traits responsible for deviant behavior may precipitate unhealthy social environments. For those whose criminality or deviance ends at adolescence, Moffitt explains that criminality subsides because social factors (for example, an unhealthy family environment) rather than biological factors were responsible for the behavior. When the interaction of biological and social conditions persist over a long period of time, it becomes difficult for a person to retract from involvement in antisocial behavior.

Richard III, as we know, was plagued by several biological abnormalities (see Chapter 7). At birth, he was different from most babies: he had teeth, which is quite unusual for a newborn, and had a crooked shape in part because of his hunched back. According to some researchers on the effects of biological abnormalities (more specifically, neurology) on deviance, many violent criminals and other deviants have been diagnosed with neurological defects. After studying 4,000 Danish babies, A. Raine, a psychologist at the University of Southern California in Los Angeles, concluded that an "overwhelming number of babies who suffered birth complications were also rejected by their mothers and went on to become criminals" (1994, p. 1). Raine also concludes that there is evidence that suggests that the brains of murderers function differently from those of nonmurderers, and that there is "objective evidence of the connection between brain function and criminal behavior" (p. 1). A severely deformed child (like Richard III) may not receive adequate attention and may be shunned not only by outsiders but also by the parents. Neglect may not be caused only by the child's unpleasant looks; the demands involved in caring for a handicapped child may precipitate adverse responses from the caretaker. Neglect in many instances breeds anger and hostility in a child.

Almost everyone in Richard's life was turned off by his deformity. The midwife in the delivery room mocked his physical anomalies (see discussion on social bond in Chapter 10); those who knew him heaped insults on him about his deformity (see Chapter 7); and his own mother maintained that Richard "cam'st on earth to make the earth [her hell]" (IV.iv.301) and that "a grievous burden was [his] birth to [her]" (IV.iv.302).

These declarations alone indicate the hostile social environment in which Richard lived. With persistent rejection and abuse from almost everyone, even "man's best friend" as we learn from Richard himself—"dogs bark at me as I halt by them" (I.v.26)—it is not surprising that Richard reacts negatively. Moffitt contends that "a sequence of interactions would be most likely to produce lasting antisocial behavior problems if caretaker reactions were more likely to exacerbate than to ameliorate children's problem behavior" (Moffitt 1993, p. 81).

From an early age, Richard exhibited deviant behavior as we learn from his mother, "[T]etchy and wayward was thy infancy; thy school days frightful, desperate, wild, and furious" (*Richard III*, IV.iv,168–70), and because the social environment he lived in was incessantly hostile toward him, hatred and rage became ingrained in him. He declared, "I am determined to prove a villain," and he embarked on a lifetime of criminality as evidenced by his deeds and his mother's testimonial: his "prime of manhood [was] daring, bold, and venturous" (IV.iv.307). This continuity in criminal behavior is what Moffitt refers to as "life course-persistent" behavior. Shakespeare, however, had no fancy label for this type of behavior.

There are several reasons for the persistent behavior seen in Richard. First, his biological traits remained unaltered. Richard's deformity left him with a sense of ill feeling, anger, and the urge to act out. Second, no one accepted him; indeed, no one loved him—"no one loves me, I am myself alone" (3 *Henry VI*, V.vi.101)—and so there was no need for him to show acts of love to anyone else—"I that have neither pity, love, nor fear" (V.vi.85). Third, Richard had embedded in himself the need to be respected and feared, and the way he knew best to bring this about was violence. Finally, those who tolerated him were criminals—his father and other outlawed men. Richard was surrounded by two groups: one ridiculed his looks and fed his rage; the other accepted him because he shared their criminal values.

Shakespeare's presentation of Richard and the conditions that led him to a lifetime of criminality are in line with Moffitt's explanation of "the emergence of antisocial behavior" and the persistence of that behavior.

> Early individual differences may set in motion a downhill snowball of cumulative continuities. In addition, individual differences may themselves persist from infancy to adulthood, continuing to influence adolescent and adult behavior in a proximal contemporary fashion. Contemporary continuity arises if the life course-persistent person continues to carry into adulthood the same underlying constellation of traits that got him into trouble as a child, such as high activity level, irritability, poor self-control, and low cognitive ability. (Moffitt 1993, p. 110)

The insults levied on Richard, and the rejections he encountered, caused rage to accumulate in him, and it was inevitable that he would act out aggressively. Shakespeare is thus insinuating that, when abnormal biological traits that expose a person to ridicule and shame are not corrected, the unhealthy social climate combined with low self-esteem and anger are likely to lead a person to antisocial behavior. Moffitt, writing several hundred years after Shakespeare, reasons in a similar manner:

> In nurturing environments, toddlers' problems are often corrected. However, in disadvantaged homes, schools, and neighborhoods, the responses are more likely to exacerbate than amend. Under

such detrimental circumstances, difficult behavior is gradually elaborated into conduct problems and a dearth of prosocial skills. Thus over the years, an antisocial personality is slowly and insidiously constructed. (Moffitt 1993, p. 103)

INTERACTIONAL THEORY OF DELINQUENCY: RICHARD III

Although Thornberry's interactional theory is very current, the concept of explaining delinquency through an interactive process is not unique to him. In explaining the reasons that propelled Richard III to a life of crime, a number of theoretical concepts and how they interact with one another are deciphered: weakened social bond due to (1) lack of attachment to parents and lack of commitment to and noninvolvement in meaningful activities, such as going to school; and (2) learning delinquency through prolonged association with a delinquent father and relatives who reinforce the behavior.

To explain the weakened social bond in Richard's life, Shakespeare traces Richard's life from birth. Usually, the birth of a child brings an abundance of joy and love, but Richard's birth brought pain and misery to his mother. A sense of compassion and sensitivity was absent from the earliest days of Richard's life. When he was born, Richard was considered "less than a mother's hope . . . an indigest deformed lump" (3 Henry VI, V.vi.60, 62). His abnormalities were a source of fun to those with whom he ought to have had a close relationship. His father was absent from his life, and the only acknowledgement he got from his father was in relation to his combative prowess. Richard did not have a close relationship with his siblings as can be inferred from his utterances—"I have no brother, I am like no brother" (3 Henry VI, V.vi.98)—and he was unable to get a lover because of his physical condition—[I cannot] "prove a lover" (Richard III, I.i.31). It is thus evident that his ties to significant others were weak. Those he aligned himself with were outlaws who engaged in a bloody battle to claim the throne.

Besides having a weakened bond to significant others, Richard was not involved in any meaningful activities. All he engaged in were wars to claim a throne that rightfully was not his. As we learn from his mother, "[T]etchy and wayward was thy infancy; thy school days frightful, desperate, wild, and furious" (Richard III, IV.iv.168–70). This statement suggests that Richard did not take school seriously.

In addition, based on his activities including a rampage of murders, one can conveniently conclude that Richard had no respect for, or belief in, the law. When he started his killing spree, one could rationalize that he was after the throne and thus killing "anyone who stood between [him] and the throne" (3 Henry VI, III.ii.231). This does not, however, legitimize his behavior. Why Richard continued with his killings after he had secured the throne defies any explanation. If anything, it reinforces the assertion that Richard had no belief in or respect for the law.

The interplay of these variables suggests that lack of attachment to a significant other may lead a person to associate with delinquent peers who may reinforce delinquent behavior, which in turn may lead a person to abandon any commitment to legitimate activities. With no involvement in, or commitment to, conventional activities, and with a social setting that encourages such behavior, Richard III resorted to crime. While criminality may diminish among some individuals over time, that may not be the case with those who have the habit deeply embedded in them. Richard's antisocial behavior started at an early age. By the time he reached adulthood, criminality had become so entrenched in Richard that it left him less likely to retreat from the behavior.

Thornberry (1996) explains his interactional theory by utilizing Hirschi's bond theory and learning theories. According to Thornberry, with weakened social bonds (for instance, a lack of attachment to significant others and a lack of involvement in worthwhile activities), a person is more likely to associate with delinquent peers from whom delinquency and criminality may be learned. In like manner, association with delinquent peers and involvement in delinquency may weaken social bonds. Thornberry further posits that, with a progression in age, the factors that lead people to crime change. While weakened social bonds may be instrumental in causing criminality among youths, a lack of involvement in or commitment to meaningful activities, as well as a prolonged association with deviant and criminal peers cause criminality among adults to persist over a lifetime.

This can be seen in Richard's case. As he grew up, Richard had no attachment to significant others. Since no one bothered about him, Richard was not inclined to impress anyone by doing well in school. His waywardness during his youthful ages could be associated with a lack of parental attachment. With no apparent formal education, and with no zeal to serve anyone when he reached adulthood, the option of engaging in conventional activities was inconceivable to Richard. Thornberry further asserts that variables such as gender, race, and social class may influence criminality in adults.

According to Thornberry, the influence of parents is crucial in molding behavior during the formative years. When parental involvement is not positive, a youth may be more inclined to seek acceptance from peers. When these peers are deviant but accepting, the youth is more likely to adopt their lifestyle. The embarrassment and disappointment that this new lifestyle might bring to the parents may further diminish parental attachment. Equally important is the fact that when a youth chooses delinquency, he or she is likely to drop out of school and limit his or her chances of obtaining a legitimate job. In the absence of a meaningful or legitimate occupation, the adult is likely to resort to criminality. Moreover, if the individual does not believe in, or respect, the laws of society, there is a greater chance he or she will break those laws. A process of learning criminality with peers who provide the requisite reinforcements has a mutual influence with weakened social bonds.

Thornberry suggests that the careers in crime persist because

> extensive involvement in delinquency at earlier ages feeds back upon and weakens attachment to parents and commitment to school. These variables, as well as involvement in delinquency itself, weaken later commitment to family and to conventional activities. Thus, these new variables, commitment to conventional activities and to family, are affected by the person's situation at earlier stages and do not "automatically" alter the probability of continued criminal involvement. If the initial bonds are extremely weak, the chances of new bonding variables being established to break the cycle towards criminal careers are low and it is likely that criminal behavior will continue. (Thornberry 1987, p. 889)

SUMMARY

The reasons that lead people to crime and deviance are diverse and sometimes difficult to explain. In some cases, several theories may be helpful in explaining criminality among certain individuals. Richard III, for example, became a criminal as a result of several reasons: lack of healthy ties to significant others, lack of belief in laws, absence of involvement in or commitment to conventional activities, biological anomalies, and learning through association with delinquent peers. It is this interplay of various factors that forms the basis of Moffitt's and Thornberry's theories of delinquency.

PART IV

SOCIAL CONTROL AND LEGAL ISSUES

15

The Etiology of Punishment

This chapter seeks to establish the different kinds of social control Shakespeare advocated. The goal is not to debate the appropriateness of Shakespeare's reasoning; rather, it is to explain it and to relate it to contemporary criminal justice and legal thinking.

The discussion in this chapter centers on two plays—*Measure for Measure* and *The Merchant of Venice*—because these plays, more than the others, appear to embody issues that relate directly to social control and inherent legal issues. The other four plays discussed in previous chapters are excluded from this discussion because there is little, if any, discussion of crime prevention.

The concept of "just deserts" in the omitted plays—the murderers all die tragically—contradicts Shakespeare's juristic and moral philosophy which he makes clear in *Measure for Measure* and *The Merchant of Venice*: "temper justice with mercy." If Shakespeare advocated the idea of just deserts he would more likely have expressed this view in *Measure for Measure*, a play whose title ironically suggests this viewpoint. Perhaps in those Shakespearean plays in which the murderers tragically lose their lives, Shakespeare is merely resonating the Biblical theme that he who lives by the sword dies by the sword (see, e.g., Matthew 26:52 and Revelation 13:10). Rousseau draws a similar conclusion (1981, p. 42). "Just desert" means that those who violate others' rights deserve to be punished (Von Hirsch 1976, p. 145).

Table 3
Specific Characters and Correctional Sanctions

Character	Play	Offense	Punishment
Froth	*Measure for Measure*	Vagrancy	Reprimand
Pompey	*Measure for Measure*	Serving in a disorderly trade	Warning and threat of whipping
Pompey	*Measure for Measure*	Theft	Incarceration and therapy
Angelo	*Measure for Measure*	Fornication	Pardon and marriage to aggrieved party
Claudio	*Measure for Measure*	Fornication	Pardon and marriage to aggrieved party
Shylock	*The Merchant of Venice*	Attempt to commit bodily harm	Pardon from receiving the death sentence, forfeiture of assets, conversion to Christianity

REASONS FOR PUNISHMENT

Throughout recorded history, criminals typically have had to pay for their crimes by some form of punishment. Most often, the punishment is meted out by a governmental agent. In societies where traditional rulers or other senior members of the community are vested with powers to settle disputes, the method used to enforce conformity to folkways or mores is known as informal social control. These two ways (state-imposed sanctions and traditional methods) of dealing with the criminal and crime are known respectively as formal and informal social control.

Social control pertains to "the social rules and processes which try to encourage good or useful conduct or discourage bad conduct" (Friedman 1984, p. 3, quoting D. Black 1972, p. 2). Friedman explains that social control, therefore, entails "the whole network of rules and processes which attach legal consequences to particular bits of behavior" (1984, p. 3). This means that because a person has been found guilty of committing a crime, or breaching the norms of society, he or she is given some kind of punishment as a display of disapproval and as a means of preventing the recurrence of such behavior. Our focus here is on governmental social control. Out of this process emerges the idea of official punishment.

Throughout its history, the concept of punishment has been viewed differently, as each generation adopts punishments that reflect its own religious and political beliefs, its own economic and social conditions, and its own customs. J. Rawls defines punishment as follows:

> A person is said to suffer punishment whenever he is legally de-prived of some of the normal rights of a citizen on the ground that he has violated a rule of law, the violation having been established by trial according to the due process of law, provided that the dep-rivation is carried out by the recognized legal authorities of the state, that the rule of law clearly specifies both the offense and the attached penalty, that the courts construe statutes strictly, and that the statute was on the books prior to the time of the offense. (1985, p. 71)

Out of this definition, several features of punishment can be discerned. First, punishment entails the infliction of something distasteful, some-thing painful. In explaining this, N. Walker makes the point that it is irrelevant what the recipient of the punishment feels about it (1991, p. 1). What counts is the perception of those who administer the punishment. It follows that, if the person being punished does not feel the brunt of the punishment, but those administering it are satisfied that it is indeed a punishment, then their conception is what is pertinent.

Second, punishment must be purposefully inflicted. In order to make it a "penological punishment," the punishment has to be inflicted on the accused for a specific reason, which is to redress a harm done.

Third, punishment must be inflicted by the state through a designated process. To make it a formal social control, only a designated state official may inflict the punishment. It follows that any punishment that is not inflicted by an appointee of the state is unofficial and may be disre-garded. If a thief is arrested at a crime scene and passersby throw punches at him, he cannot contend that he has received punishment for the crime. The pain inflicted is punishment; however, because the state did not authorize the passersby to administer the beatings, it cannot be construed as official punishment.

Fourth, punishment is inflicted because a crime has been committed, or a law has been breached. In organized societies, the laws indicate which behavior is unacceptable and what the consequences would be for displaying such unacceptable behavior. Therefore, the consequence of displaying antisocial behavior is punishment.

Fifth, punishment denotes society's disapproval. In order to maintain peace and order, society is governed through established laws. Hence, if any person deviates from those laws, the rest of society shows resentment by having the person punished.

Punishment is distinguished from revenge inasmuch as punishment is introduced because a law has been violated; revenge is a vindictive feeling that may arise not only because one's rights have been violated but because one may have been defeated by a rival or because one may have been made to feel bad about oneself. Walker makes the following distinction:

> Vengeful feelings are roused by injuries or insults to one's self or to others with whom one feels some bond. Punitive feelings are more disinterested. The occasion which calls for punishment must be a breach of some law or code of conduct: in the case of revenge it may be merely an insult or defeat in some legitimate rivalry. (1991, p. 4)

In discussing the features of punishment, it is important to note that some crimes do not require the presence of the elements of a crime. A person may still be punished even though that person did not possess a guilty mind (*mens rea*) or did not directly commit the guilty act (*actus reus*). Criminal offenses are defined with reference to four states of mind of the accused at the time a crime is committed. An accused's conduct could be reckless, knowing, purposeful, or negligent. However, strict liability imposes culpability on a person even in the absence of the above states of mind. Strict liability offenses impose liability without fault; that is, a person incurs liability even though no criminal harm was intended. Some offenses that are governed by the principle of strict liability are sale of liquor to minors, statutory rape, boarding a plane with a weapon, and sale of defective products, among others.

A person can also be punished even in the absence of an *actus reus*. That is, even though that person did not commit a criminal act, the *actus reus* of a subordinate may be transferred to that person (*respondeat superior*, or let the superior answer). This is possible through the principle of vicarious liability. Some examples under this principle are an owner of a bar taking responsibility for the manager's offense of violating a city ordinance with regard to closing time (*State v. Beaudry*, 1985) or the sale of liquor to minors, and parents taking responsibility for their child (for example, in 1997, Susan and Anthony Provenzino of Detroit, Michigan, were held responsible for the crimes of their son). The idea here is to show that sometimes punishment may be meted out to persons who are in the strict sense not offenders or criminals.

Rawls discusses two views on the justification of punishment. First, the retributive view holds that punishment is justified because people who do wrong deserve to be punished. They are guilty of doing something inappropriate, and it is only right that they receive an appropriate punishment. Second, the utilitarian view holds that acts that have been done are done, and only future effects are relevant to present decisions. Punishment is justifiable only if its consequences can be used to maintain social order.

The retributive view dates back to the Biblical times when paying back an evil deed with an evil deed was acceptable ("a tooth for a tooth"). According to Sir James F. Stephen, a nineteenth-century judge and historian of criminal law,

> The infliction of punishment by law gives definite expression and a solemn ratification and justification to the hatred which is excited by the commission of the offense. The criminal law thus proceeds upon the principle that it is morally right to hate criminals, and it confirms and justifies that sentiment by inflicting on criminals punishments which express it. I think it highly desireable that criminals should be hated, that the punishments inflicted upon them should be so contrived as to give expression to that hatred, and to justify it so far as the public provision of means for expressing and gratifying a healthy natural sentiment can justify and encourage it. The forms in which deliberate anger and righteous disapprobation are expressed, and the execution of criminal justice is the most emphatic of such forms, stand to the one set of passions in the same relation in which marriage stands to sexual passion. (quoted in Samaha 1996, p. 16)

Stephen, and other retributionists, contend that punishment is justified on the grounds that it gratifies society and enables the offender to atone for his or her deeds. Utilitarians, on the other hand, seek to prevent future crimes by deterring the offender and the rest of society. In addition, utilitarians approve of incapacitation because it supposedly prevents an offender while incarcerated from committing further crimes; those castrated, from being pedophiles; or those executed, from ever again committing any crime. Utilitarians also endorse rehabilitation because, it is presumed, an offender can thus be made more sociable and less likely to commit crimes.

THE ETIOLOGY OF PUNISHMENT

In ancient times, the most prevalent type of punishment was exile or banishment (Siegel 1983, p. 520). Those who were commonly subjected to the rigors of this type of punishment were slaves. A thief caught flagrante delicto was usually executed immediately. This practice was common among the Romans. Infractions like assault and arson were punished by economic sanctions. In the early Middle Ages (A.D. 500 to 1000), crimes were usually settled by feuds between the aggrieved party and the offender. Also common among the Romans at this time was the practice of informal social control, with an exchange of property as the remedial sanction. After the eleventh century, redress for infractions were either a forfeiture of land or other tangible assets. Siegel notes that it was in the twelfth century that the word "felony" (*felonia*) was coined to denote disloyalty to one's feudal lord. Around the fifteenth century, the economic, political, and social changes that took place in England and other European countries led to the institution of "capital" and "corporal" punishments to control the increasing numbers of thieves, robbers, vagrants, beggars, and other types of criminals and deviants.

In the seventeenth and eighteenth centuries, because of the increasing demands for labor in industries, corporal and capital punishments were partly abandoned in favor of forced labor. It was during this period that the Poor Laws were implemented requiring vagrants, beggars, and other members of the poor class to do forced labor. In the eighteenth and nineteenth centuries, the United States launched the first correction reform under the guidance of William Penn of Pennsylvania. After revising the Pennsylvania criminal code, such punishments as "torture, and capricious use of mutilation and physical punishments" were abandoned for incarceration with hard labor, "moderate floggings, fines, and forfeiture of property" (Siegel 1983, p. 522). It was under Penn's directives that jails similar to those of today were built.

In 1787 Dr. Benjamin Rush (a Quaker) formed the Philadelphia Society for Alleviating the Miseries of Public Prisons. The Quakers advocated the moderate use of capital punishment in cases of treason, murder, rape, and arson. In New York, the Auburn system was implemented which had as its philosophy the prevention of crime through the fear of crime with measures that included solitude and hard work.

In the twentieth century, a variety of punishments exist: capital punishment, incarceration, fines, community service, parole, and probation.

ANGELO'S APPLICATION OF THE LAW

Throughout *Measure for Measure*, repeated appeals are made for strict and impartial justice, for which Angelo, the deputy of Vienna, stands. The last scene of the play, however, reverses this stance for a more compassionate form of justice—one that is "seasoned with mercy."

In Shakespeare's time, almost every crime was punished by death including offenses that might be considered venial. No extenuating circumstances were considered. Lechery committed by two consenting adults engaged to be married was therefore punished the same as lewdness committed by strangers. Common sense dictates that the gravity of the two offenses differs and thus the punishment should differ. However, Claudio, who fornicates with his fiancée, is sentenced to death as anyone else who engaged in illicit sexual intercourse. There seems to be no justification for Claudio's punishment except to incite fear in the minds of others.

Looking at this from a contemporary viewpoint, it defies reason even to classify Claudio's conduct as criminal. Professor H. L. A. Hart's comments in his book *Punishment and Responsibility* have some bearing on this issue. He states, in regard to offenses that may be deemed venial, "A vast area of the criminal law where what is forbidden or enjoined by the law is so remote from the familiar requirements of morality that the very word 'crime' seems too emphatic a description of law breaking" (1968, p. 236). Therefore, "many modern retributivists would concede that punishment was to be justified and measured mainly by utilitarian considerations" (p. 236). It is for this reason that Shakespeare, speaking through the Duke, emphasizes the necessity for punishment to fit the crime and for judges to use sensible judgment in handling breaches of the law.

After fourteen years of passive government, the Duke entrusts Angelo with the responsibility of reviving dormant laws in order to suppress crime. Friar Thomas immediately has premonitions about Angelo's capability to execute the duties: "It rested in your grace to unloose this tied-up justice when you pleased; and it in you more dreadful would have seem'd than in Lord Angelo" (I.iii.37–40), Friar Thomas says to the Duke. Angelo's method of applying justice requires no consideration for mitigating circumstances, and no room for partiality as he declares: "We must not make a scarecrow of the law, setting it up to fear the birds of prey, and let it keep one shape till custom make it their perch, and not their terror" (II.i.1–5).

Angelo believes that by applying the letter of the law to its fullest, both the defendant and others will be deterred from similar behavior. He thus endorses deterrence both specific and general as an important function of punishment. In this case, however, Claudio cannot be deterred after he has been killed because dead people are incapacitated but not deterred.

By specific deterrence, the guilty person is impeded from further engagement in crime due to the unpleasant thought of punishment; by general deterrence, everyone is discouraged from engaging in similar behavior because of the impending punishment for breaking the law. So firm is Angelo's commitment to applying the law that he tells Isabella, "It is the law, not I condemn your brother; were he my kinsman, brother, or my son, it should be thus with him: He [Claudio] must die tomorrow" (II.ii.106–109). If he were to be soft on crime, Vienna would witness further moral degeneration. Claudio, while awaiting death, seems to agree that if the laws had been applied strictly, prostitution would not have been as widespread as it was at the time: "[F]rom too much liberty Lucio, liberty as surfeit is the father of much fast, so every scope by the immoderate use turns to restraint. Our natures do pursue—like rats that ravin down their proper bane,—a thirsty evil; and when we drink we die" (I.iii.12–17).

Angelo seems to have been acting on a misguided belief that implementing the death penalty for all types of crime will ameliorate the problems that plagued the Viennese. Perhaps if he had varied the intensity of the punishment, based on the type of offense, and the manner of execution, he might have obtained some success in his war on crime. C. Beccaria, writing on the necessity to institute punishment based on types of crime, asserts that

> there must . . . be a proper proportion between crimes and punishment. . . . If an equal punishment be ordained for two crimes that do not equally injure society, men will not be any more deterred from committing the greater crime, if they find a greater advantage associated with it. (1963, p. 63)

Claudio is the first to be sentenced under Angelo's direction. There are extenuating circumstances which, in his case, Angelo could have considered before passing sentence on Claudio: (1) Claudio's sexual encounter took place with his fiancée, (2) the act was consensual, and (3) Angelo's father was full of virtue as Escalus reminds Angelo: "[L]et us be keen, and rather cut a little than fall and bruise to death. Alas! this gentleman, whom I would save, had a most noble father . . . whom I believe to be most strait in virtue" (II.i.5–9).

Because Angelo believes in setting an example to deter others, he ignores those mitigating circumstances. He declares:

> The law hath not been dead, though it hath slept;
> Those many had not dar'd to do that evil,
> If the first man that did the edict infringe
> Had answer'd for his deed: now 'tis awake;
> Takes note of what is done; and, like a prophet,
> looks in a glass, that shows what future evils,
> Either now, or by remissness new-conceiv'd,
> And so in progress to be hatch'd and born,
> Are now to have no successive degrees,
> But where they live, to end. (II.ii.120–130)

Angelo's point typifies the sentiments of proponents of the death penalty in current times. Those who support the death penalty and the application of maximum sentences for serious offenses believe that others will be deterred from committing similar offenses. On the other hand, some writers detest the idea of sentencing people to effect deterrence because, as they contend, people are thereby used as objects. W. B. Eldridge, arguing against using people to deter others, maintains that such practices are "a violation of the most fundamental notions of human rights" (1982, p. 108). Eldridge then quotes Von Hirsch:

> While deterrence explains why most people benefit from the existence of punishment, the benefit to the many is not by itself a just basis for depriving the offender of his liberty and reputation. Some other reason then is needed to explain the suffering inflicted on the offender. (1982, p. 108)

Long before Eldridge and others had expressed the presumed immorality of using an offender to deter others, Immanuel Kant wrote,

> Judicial punishment can never be used merely as a means to promote some other good for the criminal himself or for civil society, but instead it must in all cases be imposed on him only on the ground that he has committed a crime; for a human being can never be manipulated merely as a means to the purposes of someone else and can never be confused with the objects of the law of things. (quoted in Murphy 1985, p. 21)

Shakespeare, speaking through the Duke, must have harbored these same feelings as suggested in the discussion of the Duke's punishment to Claudio. Others like J. Andenaes (1974) and H. Hart (1968), who are more gentle in their approach on using "man as a means," contend that the Kantian assertion restricts treating men only as means but that it is allright to use men as ends as long as their rights and interests are maintained (Zimring and Hawkins 1973, p. 36).

CAPITAL PUNISHMENT AND DETERRENCE

According to H. A. Bedau (1997, p. 128), Walker (1991, p. 13), and J. P. Gibbs (1975, p. 29), the word deterrence raises several difficulties. The foremost of these is the inability for some to distinguish between behavior that may be categorized as resulting from fear from that which simply arises from transferring (displacing) the acts. The point here is that it is easy for people to be misled into thinking that prospective criminals are being deterred by the law when they may instead have just changed where they commit crimes, or may have voluntarily renounced criminal behavior because of a pang of conscience, or may be incapable of "weigh-

ing the perceived risks" entailed in committing a crime. According to
Walker, penalties may not necessarily inhibit criminal behavior; extraneous factors such as "high walls, dogs, or barbed wires" may deter a
would-be offender (1991, p. 14). Although the word "deterrence" has
been conceptualized differently (see Bedau 1970, pp. 206–7; Ball 1955,
p. 347), Walker explains that "people are deterred from actions when
they *refrain* from them because they dislike what they believe to be the
possible consequences of those actions" (1991, p. 13; italics in original).
When that happens, one can thereafter conclude that deterrence has occurred.

The data suggest that making punishment for some crimes more certain and increasing the gravity of the punishment are minute deterrants
to criminal behavior, and that the certainty of punishment has a slight
edge over severity (see Cullen and Agnew 1999, p. 249). Support for this
contention comes from inmates who assert that they were not really concerned about the punishment that might be imposed if they were caught.
They believed that they would not be caught, and if they were caught,
they would get away with a lenient sentence (1999, p. 249).

Angelo, however, steadfastly believes that Claudio's death will cleanse
Vienna of incontinence as he tells Isabella who pleads for pity on her
brother's behalf:

> I show [pity] most of all when I show justice;
> For then I pity those I do not know,
> Which a dismiss'd offense would after gall,
> And do him right that, answering one foul wrong,
> Lives not to act another. Be satisfied;
> Your brother dies tomorrow: be content. (II.ii.131–37)

Angelo's logic is sound, but let us consider its effectiveness. In considering the argument for capital punishment and deterrence, D. Conway
suggests that capital punishment may actually not have the deterrent
effect it is deemed to have because, while it may deter a person of rational mind, it may not deter persons of irrational minds who, it appears,
represent a large part of the offending population (1985, pp. 125–33).
Siegel makes the same point (1983, p. 101). He submits that many acts
are committed by "people who are not in full control of their reasoning
power" because of drunkenness or drugs. It will be a mistake to think
that people with austere minds are immune from irrational behavior.

Sometimes even those credited with impeccable moral rectitude
"snap" and may behave in ways that had they given more thought to it
at the time, they would not have done what they did. Although most
people are aware of the law, knowledge and the fear of it may not deter
someone who under rage snaps.

Walker identifies different "states of mind" which may prompt conformists to become "temporarily undeterrable" and thus lapse into committing acts they otherwise would not have (1991, p. 14). The states of mind are "fear, fury, intoxication, vengefulness, sudden sexual desire" (p. 14). In addition, there are others who may not be deterred because they are mentally unstable, are on an ego trip (for example, gang members), or are on a suicide mission and thus have nothing to lose.

Conway concedes that capital punishment does not have a deterrent effect because most criminals "do not expect to be caught or they hold no expectations at all"; that is, they are acting in "blind passion" (1985, p. 127). Shakespeare makes this point in his portrayal of Angelo. When Angelo proclaims to Escalus, " 'Tis one thing to be tempted . . . another thing to fall. . . . When I, that do censure [Claudio], do so offend, let mine own judgment pattern out my death, nothing come in partial" (II.i.22–38), he is unaware that he is going to "fall" to "blind passion."

When he succumbs to temptation and solicits lewdness, ironically all his outspokenness about the deterrent effect of capital punishment does not in anyway deter him from engaging in a similar offense. Moreover, Angelo is not deterred because he believes that he will not be caught. When Isabella threatens to expose his sexual gestures, Angelo replies:

Who will believe thee, Isabel? My unsoil'd name, the austereness of my life, my vouch against you, and my place i' the state will so your accusation overweigh that you shall stifle in your own report, and smell of calumny. (II.iv.182–87)

By making Angelo the first person to solicit sex after he sentences Claudio to death for a similar offense, Shakespeare is making the point that deterrence, especially for that kind of offense, does not work. Claudio is caught for fornicating because his fiancée gets pregnant. Because sexual activities are usually carried out behind closed doors, only expectant couples or those who frequent brothels will be a target for punishment. By making Angelo the first to fornicate after he revives the death penalty for fornication, Shakespeare is asserting that people usually do not contemplate the ensuing punishment before committing a crime. They commit the crime hoping that they will not be caught.

Siegel makes the point that "positivist criminologists" suggest that many social and psychological factors affect the choices people make. Those with a "strong stake in society" may be deterred more than those with economic, social, family, educational, and other problems" (1983, p. 102). To some, just the fear of being stigmatized is sufficient deterrence. One may assume that Angelo was afraid of the stigma but, because he believed that he would never be exposed, the thought of being stigmatized did not cross his mind. Angelo, as deputy to the Duke, had a "stake in society" but he is not deterred by the law. It therefore follows that deterrence may be effected only by a combination of other variables.

Some studies regarding the deterrent effect of the death penalty have been heavily criticized for methodological flaws. They fail to provide any credence to the understanding on this issue (see Ehrlich 1973, 1975; Layson 1985). Studies conducted by Zimring and Hawkins (1986), Bedau (1967, 1982), and Sellin (1967, 1980) all failed to produce a nexus between the death penalty and deterrence. Bedau has concluded that there is no known research that indicates that capital punishment deters capital murders (1997, p. 154).

Some contend that when capital punishment is made certain and implemented speedily, people will be more likely to be deterred from engaging in felonies that require the death penalty (Jeffrey 1965; Beccaria 1963). According to Jeffrey,

> The uncertainty of capital punishment is one major factor in the system. Another factor is the time element. A consequence [the death penalty] must be applied immediately if it is to be effective. . . . The lesson to be learned from capital punishment is not that punishment does not deter, but that the improper and sloppy use of punishment does not deter or rehabilitate. (1965, p. 299)

Although the literature on the causal effects of the celerity of executions and deterrence is scanty, W. Bailey and R. Peterson found no evidence to support the hypothesis that "speedy executions discourage murder" (1994, p. 24). Certainly, Shakespeare had given thought to this issue. While Angelo contemplates having Claudio put to death the next day, the certainty and celerity of the execution do not deter him for, as we know, he solicits lechery before the supposed execution is carried out.

Another point of importance here is that Angelo seems to have implemented the maximum penalty not so much to punish the offense but to deter others. When a punishment which is more severe than should be is imposed, other issues are generated. In particular, when the offense is minimal and is not a threat to society (as Claudio's), people are apt to regard the justice system as unfair.

PROCEDURAL ISSUES

The Bill of Rights in the United States Constitution embodies some guarantees and immunities that limit the federal government's powers so that the rights and privileges of the individual are not abrogated. In 1791, when these amendments were incorporated into the U.S. Constitution, it was clear that the first eight amendments were, in a strict sense, not binding on the states. In 1868 wordings of the Fifth Amendment regarding "due process" were made binding on the states through the Fourteenth Amendment. The Fifth and Fourteenth Amendments, among other things, state that no one shall be "deprived of life, liberty, and property without due process of law." Although the words seem straightforward, they have been subjected to various interpretations by the courts over the years. Essentially, the clause is intended to protect certain fundamental rights of an individual based on a balancing of the government's interest. With regard to the Fourteenth Amendment, the due process clause extends many of the protections of the Bill of Rights to the states.

Some of the provisions of the Bill of Rights which are applicable both to the federal and the state governments and which have direct relevance to the discussion in this section are the Sixth and Eighth Amendments. The Sixth Amendment guarantees an accused the right to a "jury of one's peers" and a "compulsory process for obtaining witnesses in his favor, and to have the assistance of Counsel for his defense." In addition, the Eighth Amendment prohibits "cruel and unusual punishment." It follows that no law should be "unreasonable," "arbitrary," or "capricious."

The objective of procedural fairness is that an accused whose life, liberty, or property is at stake is given an opportunity to present his or her case fully. These guarantees, which exist in common law, were transplanted to the United States by the founding fathers. Many of these due process clauses were written in the U.S. Constitution in 1791, almost two centuries after Shakespeare wrote *Measure for Measure* and *The Merchant of Venice* in which he discusses the necessity for compliance to those procedural requirements.

DUE PROCESS

Two main issues in regard to procedural rights are discerned from Claudio's case: (1) Claudio was deprived of due process of the law and (2) the law under which he was charged was "unreasonable" and "arbitrary." As we discuss the law in Shakespeare's plays, it is important to know that, although the settings of some plays were in different countries, the law Shakespeare applied was English law (see Keeton 1967).

Angelo refused to take into account facts that mitigate against Claudio's offense even after a solemn plea from Escalus, his deputy:

Ay, but yet let us be keen, and rather cut a little
Than fall and bruise to death. Alas! this gentleman,
Whom I would save, had a most noble father.
Let but your honor know,
Whom I believe to be most strait in virtue,

> That in the working of your own affections,
> Had time coher'd with place, or place with wishing,
> Or that the resolute acting of your blood
> Could have attain'd the effect of your own purpose,
> Whether you had not sometime in your life
> Err'd in this point which now you censure him,
> And pull'd the law upon you. (II.i.6–21)

In addition to the fact that Claudio's act was consensual with his fiancée, Escalus makes it clear that because of his father's good deeds and because it was a venial offense that even Angelo was guilty of Claudio's life should be spared. The fact that Claudio needed Isabella to intercede on his behalf supposes the need for counsel for the defendant. This is another procedural right Claudio was deprived of. This deprivation stemmed out of the practice that existed in England prior to 1688. Misdemeanants were entitled to legal representation but, curiously, felons were denied that privilege. The English revolution of 1688 relaxed that harshness for felons who committed treason; and in 1836, the English parliament extended the right to counsel to all felons. It can be presumed that the legislators in England at the time (and Shakespeare before them) viewed the denial of counsel to felons as a means by which abuses within the justice system could be perpetrated. In the United States, even before the right to counsel was incorporated into the U.S. Constitution in 1791, the original thirteen states had provisions to that effect added to their own constitutions.

The repercussions when counsel is absent in criminal matters are enormous. Justice Sutherland's comments in *Powell v. Alabama* (the Scottsboro case), 287 U.S. 45 (1932), eloquently summarizes these repercussions.

> The right to be heard would be, in many cases, of little avail if it did not comprehend the right to be heard by counsel. Even the intelligent and educated layman has small and sometimes no skill in the science of law. If charged with crime, he is incapable, generally, of determining for himself whether the indictment is good or bad. He is unfamiliar with the rules of evidence. Left without the aid of counsel he may be put on trial without proper charge, and convicted upon incompetent evidence, or evidence irrelevant to the issue or otherwise inadmissible. He lacks both the skill and knowledge adequately to prepare his defense, even though he has a perfect one.

Claudio, a victim of these consequences, is incapable of arguing the indictment against him. Had he had counsel, the latter would have been able to establish that the charge against Claudio was bad because it was baseless. Assuming *arguendo* that sexual intercourse with one's fiancée is evil, counsel would have argued that Claudio be charged with a misdemeanor and not a felony because having consensual sexual intercourse with one's betrothed is in no way injurious to society as is the case with indiscriminate lewdness. It follows that counsel would have portrayed the gross disproportionality between the offense and the punishment.

In 1963, in the case of *Gideon v. Wainwright*, 372 U.S. 335 (1963), the U.S. Supreme Court held that the government had to provide indigent defendants with counsel in all felony trials. In the case of *Argersinger v. Hamlin*, 407 U.S. 25 (1972), the Supreme Court made it clear that "absent a knowing and intelligent waiver, no person may be imprisoned for any offense, whether classified as petty, misdemeanor, or felony unless he was represented by counsel at his trial."

The Duke's reversal of Angelo's decision implies that Shakespeare had considered the necessity for the observation of due process of the law.

Modern courts, especially when faced with death penalty cases, consider the failure to look into all aspects of an offender's case a breach of the Eighth Amendment which rejects "cruel and unusual punishment." In discussing the case of *Lockett v. Ohio*, 438 U.S. 586, (1978), a case which deals with the death penalty, M. J. Radin states the merit of the court's decision in considering due process:

> Chief Justice Burger reasoned that the "degree of respect due the uniqueness of the individual" renders execution a cruel punishment if sentence is imposed under statute limiting the scope of evidence that the defendant may offer in mitigation of her crime. (1985, pp. 134–35)

Radin further explains that the death penalty is validated "if imposed under procedural statutes that guide the sentencer's discretion by directing the sentencer to weigh aggravating and mitigating factors" (p. 135). She also makes the point that "a process, not just the event it authorizes, can be considered cruel in the constitutional sense" (p. 135).

The Viennese law, as applied by Angelo, limited the scope of evidence that Claudio could have produced to exculpate himself from criminal liability. In fact, the law made no provision for a defendant to introduce any evidence that might help his or her case. The whole process was so coercive and so cruel as to prohibit the benefits of counsel, preclude the consideration of mitigating factors, and completely ignore the principle of proportionality.

In the United States, the death penalty remains a controversial issue. In the case of *Furman v. Georgia*, 408 U.S. 238 (1972), thirty-seven states observed a moratorium while reviewing the way in which the death penalty was arbitrarily and capriciously imposed as a result of the absence of a guided process. Some states proposed a process which will require fact finders to take into consideration aggravating and mitigating circumstances. In *Gregg v. Georgia*, 428 U.S. 242 (1976), this new procedure was tested. A bifurcated process was adopted which requires first a guilt or innocence phase and second a penalty phase. During the penalty phase, the jury takes into consideration mitigating and aggravating circumstances. When considering mitigating circumstances, several factors, such as the defendant's character, age, work ethics, and other qualities that may be established to evoke leniency, are introduced. Factors that may aggravate a defendant's sentence include whether the murder resulted while the defendant was committing a felony, whether the victim was an officer of the law, whether several lives were endangered. The Supreme Court has also determined that not all felonies require the death penalty. For instance, in *Coker v. Georgia*, 433 U.S. 584 (1977), the Court determined that the death penalty was not a proportionate punishment for the offense of rape. It follows that when there is no loss of life, the courts are likely to consider the death penalty for such an offense cruel and unusual punishment.

When, later in the play, the Duke resumes power and reverses Angelo's decision, he acts in compliance with the mandate of due process. Once again, we see Shakespeare ahead of his time.

Claudio's case was not the only one brought before Angelo. He also considered the cases of Froth and Pompey. Because these seemed to be relatively trivial, however, he left Escalus to "find good cause to whip them all" (II.i.155).

Escalus, who advocates mercy and respect for due process in applying the law, considers a reprimand an appropriate method of disciplining Froth: "Master Froth, I would not have you acquainted with tapsters: they will draw you, Master Froth, and you will hang them. Get you gone, and let me hear no more of you" (II.i.228–29). The reprimand appeared to be effective because we do not hear about him thereafter. Pompey, the clown, does nothing at first except work in a disreputable business. Escalus reprimands and threatens him with a whipping:

> I advise you, let me not find you before me again upon any complaint whatsoever, no, not for dwelling where you do; if I do, Pompey, I shall beat you to your tent, and prove a shrewd Caesar to you; in plain dealing, Pompey, I shall have you whipt: so for this time, Pompey, fare you well. (II.i.271–78)

The reprimand is ineffective because Pompey later steals. This time he is brought before the Duke.

SUMMARY

The concept of punishment and its functions are outlined in the early pages of the chapter. Throughout history, each generation has implemented different types of punishments in an effort to ameliorate crime. Angelo's method of applying the law, together with the outcome of unmitigated justice, is examined in light of social control. Angelo, the interim duke, held the conservative view that by implementing stern sanctions people will be deterred from committing crimes. He orders the death penalty for Claudio who admits to fornicating with his fiancée. Angelo solicits sex from Claudio's sister who is interceding on Claudio's behalf. Angelo fornicates with his estranged betrothed whom he mistakenly believes to be Isabella, Claudio's sister. Shakespeare thus makes the point that the death penalty is not an effective deterrent.

The rights of the accused in the judicial system are examined. It is important, as Shakespeare suggests, that an accused be given certain rights throughout the judicial process.

16

The Duke's Judgment

The Duke's approach to redressing a wrong contrasts sharply to Angelo's. The following statements represent the Duke's stance: (1) punishment must be proportionate to the crime; (2) mitigating and aggravating circumstances must be considered; (3) justice should be tempered with mercy; and (4) incarceration and therapy must go together.

After the Duke regains the power he earlier vested in Angelo, he sets about to reverse Angelo's decisions. Instead of meting out punishment by the strict letter of the law, the Duke takes into account the special characteristics of each offender, noting extenuating or aggravating circumstances. Following the law in the strict sense, Pompey would be sentenced to death as Elbow the constable reminds us, "[H]is neck will come to your waist, a cord, sir" (III.ii.44). However, because the Duke considers the crime somewhat trivial, he settles for a lesser punishment. Pompey is to be incarcerated and given some counseling: "Take him to prison, officer; correction and instruction must both work ere this rude beast will profit" (III.ii.34–35). The Duke's reasoning, as Keeton suggests, is that to execute Pompey would be "needless cruelty" but by separating him from bad company he could with some discipline become "an honest, if un-intelligent, citizen" (1967, p. 389). Moreover, the Duke believes that with counseling the likelihood of Pompey relapsing will be somewhat diminished. To become an honest citizen, as the Duke would want, Pompey must be rehabilitated through therapy. Shakespeare discussed the need for counseling even before it was recognized as a form of treatment. Counseling was recommended not only to help Pompey be a more sociable human, but also to provide him with job skills so that he might become a more productive member of society.

The therapeutic approach has received much attention in current times within the criminal justice system. Some believe that treatment can rehabilitate criminals to function well in society; others are bothered that the therapeutic approach fails to address general deterrence.

Karl Menninger, a proponent for the therapeutic approach, discusses his stance on therapy:

> If we were to follow scientific methods, the convicted offender would be detained indefinitely pending a decision as to whether and how and when to reintroduce him successfully into society. All the skill and knowledge of modern behavioral science would be used to examine his personality assets, his liabilities and potentialities, the environment from which he came, its effects upon him, and his effects upon it.
>
> Having arrived at some diagnostic grasp of the offender's personality, those in charge can decide whether there is a chance that he can be redirected into a mutually satisfactory adaptation to the world. If so, the most suitable techniques in education, industrial training, group administration, and psychotherapy should be selectively applied. All this may be best done extramurally or intramurally. It may require maximum "security" or only minimum "security." If, in due time, perceptible change occurs, the process should be expedited by finding a suitable spot in society and industry for him, and getting him out of prison control and into civil status (with parole control) as quickly as possible. (1985, p. 175)

In R. Wasserstrom's discussion of the debate on the therapeutic approach, he incorporates the views of Lady Barbara Wooton, an outspoken advocate for the therapeutic approach, and those of H. L. A. Hart, an opponent of the approach (1985, pp. 190–97). Wooton proposes the elimination of the idea of the guilty mind (*mens rea*) to determine culpability. She argues that a punitive system should be eliminated and a totally rehabilitative system instituted for all types of criminals. The criminal is sick, she contends, so we ought to treat rather than punish him or her (p. 194). The problem here, as Wasserstrom explains, is that not all criminal acts are caused by those we consider sick (e.g., those with compulsive disorders and insane persons). Absent proof that all offenders are sick, treatment cannot be proposed for all offenders.

On the other hand, Hart worries that because the approach does not take into consideration general deterrence, it is not a "justifying aim of a system of punishment":

The objection to assigning to Reform this place in punishment is not merely that punishment entails suffering and reform does not; but that Reform is essentially a remedial step for which ex hypothesi there is an opportunity only at the point where the criminal law has failed in its primary task of securing society from the evil which breach of the law involves. Society is divisible at any moment into two classes (i) those who have actually broken a given law and (ii) those who have not yet broken it but may. To take Reform as the dominant objective would be to forego the hope of influencing the second—and in relation to the more serious offences—numerically much greater class. We should thus subordinate the prevention of first offences to the prevention of recidivism. (Hart quoted in 1985, p. 197)

Angelo, the deputy who solicits sex, has several factors that aggravate his case: (1) his offense is premeditated. He had time to think over his action and deal with his sexual urges, but because he thought he could get away with the crime, he went ahead and did it. (2) He misused his powers. He was an officer of the law charged with the responsibility of administering justice, and he abused that trust. (3) He concocts a plot to cover up his offense by ordering the death of Claudio, thereby breaking his part of the bargain with Isabella. (4) He had for selfish reasons called off marriage plans with Mariana and had attempted to destroy her reputation. The Duke, however, pardons him on condition that he marry Mariana. Keeton states that by bringing about this union, the Duke is upholding one of the "objects of modern criminal law—redress of the harm done" (1967, p. 392).

In Claudio's case, the Duke exercised mercy and pardoned him. The Duke must have taken into account the extenuating circumstances discussed above. Keeton, who discusses the necessity for the courts to take into consideration extenuating circumstances, notes that common law, unlike private law, has to consider both the "moral responsibility" and the "social interest" of the community: "It is one of the superior features of the common law that it is ruled by the state itself and for that reason possesses in the institution of mercy a corrective for the ruthless harshness of the law" (p. 393).

JUDICIAL ETHICS

Angelo's character raises the issue of ethical standards among persons entrusted with public trust. They, more than anyone else, are expected to conduct themselves with the utmost respectability, dedication, and dignity. This higher standard of conduct emanates from the fact that they serve the interests of the whole society and are placed in such positions

because they are considered to be qualified for them. Judges, in particular, are appointed or promoted not only because of their outstanding
service, but also because they are deemed to possess more integrity than
others.

Angelo, whose character prompts the discussion of ethics, was not
referred to as a judge, but his duties as deputy duke granted him the
power to sit in judgment of others. Technically, therefore, he was a judge.
In discussing the ethics of public service, Souryal cites the farewell address of George Washington in September 1796 (1992, pp. 94–102). Although Washington equated the virtues of public service with "the
sacredness of a public trust," he also was mindful of the "fallibility" of
public employees. He emphasized that public trust is based on "good
intentions" and the "very best exertions of men."

Angelo was delegated to cleanse Vienna of iniquity because the Duke
felt that he had the integrity to carry out the responsibility: "Lord Angelo
is precise; stands at a guard with envy; scarce confesses that his blood
flows, or that his appetite is more to bread than stone" (I.iv.59–62). Although the Duke felt that his choice of Angelo was the right one, he also
gave thought to the likelihood of his fallibility: "[H]ence shall we see, if
power change purpose, what our seemers be" (I.iv.62–63). When the
Duke summons Angelo in order to brief him about his assignment, he
tells Angelo that "there is a kind of character in thy life that to the
observer doth thy history fully unfold" (I.i.30–32). Based upon the un-
folding of Angelo's character, Shakespeare's view of the nature of the
judge's role emerges.

That Angelo is dedicated to his job and has all good intentions to
follow the strict letter of the law is indisputable: "It is the law, not I,
condemn your brother; were he my kinsman, brother, or my son, it
should be thus with him: He must die tomorrow" (II.ii.105–8). That he
is aware of the higher moral standards to which he is subjected by virtue
of his duties is evident in his own words: "[Y]ou may not so extenuate
[Claudio's] offence for I have had such faults; but rather tell me, when
I, that censure him, do so offend, let mine own judgment pattern out my
death, and nothing come partial" (II.i.34–38).

S. Goldman describes eight qualities that a good judge must possess,
three of which are directly relevant to a discussion of Angelo: (1) fair-
mindedness—a sensitivity to the requirements of procedural due process
as a means to a fair trial; (2) personal integrity—high moral standards
and an ability to withstand political and economic pressures and carry
out the law to the best of his or her ability; and (3) ability to handle
judicial power sensibly (Goldman 1982, pp. 113–14). These three qualities
are considered in appraising Angelo's character.

(1) *Fair-mindedness.* To be fair to all parties of a case, a judge must
examine the "totality of the evidence" which may include exculpating

or inculpating facts or extenuating or aggravating facts. A judge must be able to be objective and open-minded about the facts of a case. He or she must try to create equilibrium on both sides of a case. A judge must insist that both the prosecution and defense abide by court rules and the law. It follows that a judge who advocates discipline and fairness must be a symbol of discipline and fairness; and if he or she is unable to be objective then he or she should recuse himself or herself from presiding over a case.

Angelo showed neither fairness nor discipline; in his position, the honorable thing to do was to resign. It was not due to an excusable oversight that Angelo failed to consider the mitigating circumstances in Claudio's case because Escalus, his deputy, reminded him of those circumstances. His failure to respect due process was perhaps due to overzealousness and possibly lack of judicial expertise. One can detect traces of his zealousness in his response to Escalus' request for him to consider mitigating circumstances in Claudio's case:

> 'Tis one thing to be tempted, Escalus,
> Another thing to fall. I not deny
> The jury, passing on the prisoner's life,
> May in the sworn twelve have a thief or two
> Guiltier than him they try. What's open
> . . . Made to justice,
> That justice seizes. What knows the laws
> That thieves do pass on thieves? (II.i.22–29)

(2) *Personal integrity.* In this quality Angelo fails woefully. He more than anyone else ought to conduct himself with exemplary behavior, but even before the criminal he has just sentenced to die is executed, Angelo commits a similar offense. He uses his position to pass a corrupt judgment in exchange for sexual satisfaction; even worse, he does not then honor his part of the bargain. He asks regardless for Claudio's execution. The Duke speaks on the integrity of an official of the law:

> He who the sword of heaven will bear
> Should be as holy as severe;
> Pattern in himself to know,
> Grace to stand, and virtue go;
> More nor less to other paying,
> Than by self-offences weighing.
> Shame to him whose cruel striking
> Kills for faults of his own liking!
> Twice treble shame on Angelo,

To weed my vice and let his grow!
O, what may man within him hide,
Though angel on the outward side! (III.ii.287–98)

Escalus also speaks out on Angelo's fall: "I am sorry one so learned and so wise as you, Lord Angelo, have still appear'd should slip so grossly, both in the heat of blood and lack of temper'd judgment afterward" (V.i.578–81).

(3) *Ability to handle judicial power sensibly.* Goldman suggests that to handle judicial power sensibly, a judge should consider "civil rights and civil liberties and with a particular sensitivity to . . . the rights of the underdogs of society" (Goldman 1982, p. 114). Claudio was an underdog who did not receive Angelo's judicial sensitivity.

MERCY, JUSTICE, AND CRIMINAL LAW

Measure for Measure and *The Merchant of Venice* deal extensively with the concept of mercy in the application of the law. Although mercy denotes compassion which is an attitude, Walker describes mercy as "an action" and forgiveness as an "attitude" (1991, p. 115). As an action, a person or the justice system responds to the offender based on the offender's contrition or some other extenuating circumstance. As clear as this seems, retributivists and utilitarians differ in their outlook on the issue. Retributivists view mercy as a concept which should not be applicable in a court of law or in a forum legislated by a legitimate government: when mercy is applied in a justice system, it tilts the balance of justice. Utilitarians, on the other hand, hold that if the exercise of mercy would cause lesser suffering to the offender and those close to him, then it is necessary for the courts to show mercy. In *The Merchant of Venice*, Portia, the trial lawyer, in an attempt to evoke a change of mind from Shylock, reminds him of the virtues of mercy:

The quality of mercy is not strain'd;
It droppeth as the gentle rain from heaven
Upon the place beneath: it is twice bless'd;
It blesseth him that gives and him that takes:
'Tis mightiest in the mightiest; it becomes
The throned monarch better than his crown;
His sceptre shows the force of the temporal power,
The attribute to awe and majesty,
Wherein doth sit the dread and fear of kings;
But mercy is above this scepter'd sway,
It is enthoned in the heart of kings,
It is an attribute to God himself;

And earthly power doth then show likest God's
When mercy seasons justice. Therefore, Jew,
Though justice be thy plea consider this,
That in the course of justice, none of us
Should see salvation: we do pray for mercy;
And that same prayer doth teach us all to render
The deeds of mercy. (IV.i.203–21)

Portia's lengthy appeal is intended to evoke a sense of mercy from
Shylock who insists on carving out a pound of flesh from Antonio's
chest. Mercy from Shylock would require him to put aside the terms of
his bargain, with Antonio and instead accept thrice the amount of money
owed him by Antonio. The question arises why Portia, who so eloquently
pleads to Shylock to have mercy on Antonio, does not show Shylock
mercy but instead forces him to convert from Judaism to Christianity.
This is where Portia errs because, by forcing Shylock to convert to Christianity, she in essence endorses anti-Semitism. It is hypocritical that Portia who earlier had made a fervent appeal for "us all to render deeds of
mercy" lacks tolerance for people of a different race and religious orientation. It appears that in Shakespearean times, Jews were considered
an "unkind" people as one infers from Antonio's remark: "Hie thee,
gentle Jew; This Hebrew will turn Christian: he grows kind" (I.iii.197–
99). (This remark was made after Shylock finally agreed to lend Antonio
3,000 ducats.) Perhaps Portia had the same conception of Jews. Perhaps
she thought that, by forcing Shylock to become a Christian, he would
thereafter be inclined to render deeds of mercy.

In *Measure for Measure*, Isabella makes a similar appeal for mercy when
she pleads to Angelo for her brother's life:

Well believe this,
No ceremony that to great one 'longs,
Not the king's crown, nor the deputed sword,
The Marshal's truncheon, nor the judge's robe,
Become them with one half so good a grace
As mercy does.
If he had been as you, you as he,
You would have slipp'd like him; but he like you,
Would have been so stern. (II.ii.82–89)

J. G. Murphy deciphers from the two speeches above five views of
mercy: (1) it is an autonomous moral virtue; (2) it is a virtue that tempers
or "seasons" justice; (3) it is never owed to anyone as a right or a matter
of desert or justice; (4) as a moral virtue, it derives its value at least in
part from the fact that it flows from a certain kind of character—a char-

acter disposed to perform merciful acts from love or compassion while not losing sight of the importance of justice; and (5) it requires a general retributive outlook on punishment and responsibility (Murphy and Hampton 1990, p. 166).

Although these virtues of mercy are quite plausible, they raise another issue: how can mercy be shown to one person without showing some injustice to another person? It is this apparent paradox which gives rise to this discussion. Murphy reasons that, in criminal law in particular, a showing of mercy to the offender creates an injustice to the aggrieved party: "if mercy requires a tempering of justice, then there is a sense in which mercy may require a departure from justice" because "temperings are tamperings" (p. 167). It follows from his reasoning that a plea for mercy on behalf of someone who actually does something wrong is a plea for the judge to be "unjust." It would, as Murphy suggests, be "a vice, not a virtue, to manifest injustice" (p. 167). Judges are hired, he contends, to uphold the law, to "do justice"—an obligation they take an oath to do. It would be wrong therefore for them, for mercy's sake, to depart from their obligation. An imbalance in the "scales of justice" is created if people are not given what they deserve. When one commits a wrong toward another, one has created an injustice toward that other. To restore an equilibrium, the offender is given his or her due which is justice. It is irrelevant that the offender is remorseful; a judge cannot and should not absolve him or her from responsibility. It would be an affront to the law and the principles of equity if that were done.

Murphy buttresses his line of reasoning with an excerpt from *Measure for Measure*, which shows that Shakespeare had also given thought to the "other side" of mercy: "I show [pity] most of all when I show justice; for then I pity those I do not know, which a dismissed offense would after gall; and do him right that, answering one foul wrong, lives not to act another" (II.ii.131–35). Murphy's explanation of Angelo's reply to Isabella's plea for mercy is that a judge who renders a decision based on an offender's plight is ignoring the fact that his job is to "uphold an entire system of justice that protects the security of all citizens" (p. 168).

Murphy also differentiates between mercy and justice: justice demands "individuation," that is, that moral differences between people be considered and like cases be treated the same. "Judges or lawmakers who are unmindful of the importance of individuational response are not lacking in mercy; they lack a sense of justice" (p. 172). This is precisely what Angelo lacked—a sense of justice in employing due process in Claudio's case.

Murphy finally concedes that it can be all right for judges to show mercy in criminal cases "if" they are simply exercising the will of those victimized by the offender. If, by a consensus, victims express the wish to retract the prerogative they have to make sure the criminal is punished, a judge can exercise this will of the victims. The mercy thereafter shown to an offender must be based on a valid reason; for example, "compassion and love" which would make the mercy "appropriate." This ties in with Claudio's plight. Since Claudio's fiancée admitted that the sexual liaison was consensual, one would think that Claudio should escape punishment. It follows that Angelo should have shown mercy on Claudio because his victim did not want him to be punished.

MERCY, JUSTICE, AND PRIVATE LAW

The private law paradigm of mercy exemplified in *The Merchant of Venice* is, as Murphy notes, "radically" different from the discussion of mercy in criminal law cases. Murphy examines only the civil law aspect of this play. In his analysis of mercy as it relates to civil suits, Murphy contends that a judge

> does not have an antecedent obligation, required by the rules of justice, to impose harsh treatment. He rather has, in a case like Shylock's, a right to impose harsh treatment. Thus, if he chooses to show mercy, he is simply waiving a right that he could in justice claim—not violating an obligation demanded by justice. (p. 176)

Shylock's case against Antonio is a civil suit to recover a debt. It becomes criminal only when Shylock attempts to commit bodily harm by cutting flesh from Antonio's chest. It follows from the previous discussion of mercy and justice that, at the end of *The Merchant of Venice* when the Duke decides not to implement the death penalty on Shylock for conspiring to take the life of a citizen, he was exercising justice not mercy. He was exercising justice in the sense that the life of Antonio had not, after all, been taken. Reasoned differently, although the Duke waived the right to impose the death penalty on Shylock, it was not a sentence that he was obligated to impose. Since Shylock did not take his pound of flesh from Antonio, there was no antecedent criminal wrongdoing that warranted the death penalty. Hence, the Duke's mercy may be considered the right to impose the death penalty, which he waived.

EQUITY IN *THE MERCHANT OF VENICE*

Equity is "natural, ethical justice" (Rush 1986, p. 89). The doctrine of equity as a system of justice originated from the practices of the Chancery court of England. Prior to 1873 in England, only the Chancery court exercised equity, so those who sought equity had to take their case to the Chancery court. People who had their cases heard in other courts, for instance, the Court of Common Pleas, were not guaranteed equity.

When Shakespeare penned *The Merchant of Venice*, he was speaking to the necessity of all courts to administer equity. M. E. Andrews notes that, through the use of equitable devices, Shakespeare derived the following results: (1) he spared the lives of Antonio and Shylock and (2) he provided for each of them during Shylock's life and preserved the corpus of the estate for the ultimate use and benefit of Shylock's heirs (1965, p. 77). It is believed that the decision in *Glanvill v. Courtney* (1615), an actual case with facts similar to those of the case involving Shylock and Antonio, was influenced by the outcome of Shylock's case.

Shakespeare extols the following equitable devices: compliance with due process of the law, knowledge of the law and of a case before the court, fair-mindedness, neutrality with regard to the litigants, personal integrity, rational temperament, and a sense of individuation.

SUMMARY

The Duke is an advocate of due process. More insightful than Angelo, he sees the necessity for tailoring punishment to fit the crime and the criminal. Although he does not oppose incarceration, he recognizes that, if an inmate is not provided counseling, he or she is likely to relapse.

The importance of judicial ethics is emphasized. If judges are to stand in judgment of others, they must be exemplary in their own behavior. Judges should not preach what they do not or will not practice.

It is noted that the application of "mercy" in criminal suits raises the issue of whether justice is served if the judge exercises mercy toward the offender. Because the judge is not required by the rules of justice to impose harsh treatment in civil suits, he can exercise his right not to impose a harsh ruling.

Finally, the doctrine of equity is examined. In the discussion, it is made clear that the doctrine of equity, which was practiced only in the Chancery courts, is now practiced in all courts.

17

Conclusion and Recommendation

There are some important revelations to be gleaned from this study. First, it is evident that, in Shakespeare's time, as today, crime was a serious concern and no form of punishment effectively curbed it. Second, many of the crimes that exist today were also widespread in Shakespearean times. Third, and very important, it is possible to deduce from his writings that Shakespeare was a criminological theorist. Twelve criminological theories or perspectives are found in just six of his plays. Perhaps others can be found in the rest of his works.

Fourth, Shakespeare long ago recognized the necessity and importance of therapy and counseling in addressing criminality, even before the practice was officially adopted as a method of addressing lawbreaking. Fifth, he introduced the ongoing debate about whether the death penalty was an effective deterrent or a morally acceptable punishment. Sixth, Shakespeare long ago recognized that punishment should fit the crime; it was needless cruelty to execute people for petty offenses like simple theft or for inappropriate behavior such as a premarital sexual encounter.

Seventh, Shakespeare had observed the necessity of applying due process of law. He realized the necessity of the litigants to present their cases fully, to get legal representation in trials, and for laws to be reasonable and not unduly severe. Eighth, Shakespeare recognized the necessity for judges and other public officials to be ethical in the administration of their duties. Finally, Shakespeare recognized that the doctrine of equity did not have to be a practice reserved for special courts; it was mandatory for all courts.

Some may contend that because of the author's exposure or awareness of contemporary criminological theories, the characters are interpreted in that light. The important thing to remember is that the interpretations of the plays are not imagined; they are apparent. It follows that the theories that are found in the plays precede any interpretations that are now given to them.

Some analyses in this book are limited, unfortunately but not because of a lack of material. These limitations are inherent in studies that involve a broad range of issues where in-depth analysis is usually traded for brevity. Obviously, some readers may differ in their interpretations. It is inevitable in studies in which the researcher is constrained by a subjective relationship with a document. Nevertheless, in just six plays most of the major criminological theories were discovered.

Additionally, to keep this book within a reasonable length, the sample was necessarily made relatively small. As a result, certain kinds of crimes and abhorrent behavior were not given attention. The absence of these made it impossible to extend the coverage of certain theories of crime and social control. It is for these reasons that the author makes the following recommendations to anyone who intends to engage in a similar study or elaborate on some aspect of this book.

First, it would be worthwhile and significant to study the cultural setting of Shakespeare's work; the sociocultural factors that shaped the literature as well as crime and justice in the sixteenth century need to be explored. Another fascinating topic may be an examination of notorious crimes and criminals of Shakespeare's day, comparing them to those of the twentieth century. The whole idea of a comparative study on historical events as depicted in books or movies is likely to receive favorable feedbacks. Literary writers, as was discussed in Chapter 1, were the precursors in writing about crime and criminals. In such an inquiry, it would be enlightening to discuss medieval conceptions of nature as the source of a barbaric or civil society. In particular, it would be extremely informative to contextualize Shakespeare's works as they reflect criminality. In such an approach, Shakespeare would be within the social and historical context in which he wrote and described numerous scenarios of crime and justice. This author touched on this aspect, but much is left undone. In discussing the benefits of interdisciplinary perspectives of Shakespeare's works, among other things, R. Shafer points out that "when one has a solid grasp of the history of a given era and of its key people, he is able to understand an artist's interpretive rendition of that period" (1976, p. 3).

Second, specialized topics using Shakespearean plays are likely to stimulate thought processes within the disciplines of criminology, law, and criminal justice. A wide array of topics discussed in the criminal justice curriculum may be enhanced by examining fictional works. Suggestions for specialized topics include female offenders and deviants, spousal abuse, violent sexual offenders, social control with emphasis on the concept of punishment, capital punishment and deterrence, revenge, rehabilitation, incapacitation, and due process of the law.

It is a major premise of this book that the analysis of literature enriches teaching and enhances student understanding. Classical literature, perhaps next to visual aids, leaves a greater impression on students' minds than the laborious and tedious conventional text materials. The point is not in any way to discount the worth of text materials; rather that students of criminology and criminal justice should expand the range of their concerns while emphasizing textbook summaries of criminological theories. Since the discipline of criminology is still borrowing ideas from other disciplines to better understand criminals and their crimes, it makes sense to look for knowledge in all avenues, especially in the plays of one of the world's greatest writers. Innumerable fictional works, published from different periods and different civilizations, may provide us with valuable insights without detracting from the objectives of the discipline of criminology.

> It is important to recognize that integration does not mean adding one more thing to an already crowded curriculum. Rather, it provides a different way of looking at what is already scheduled to be taught. This resembles a jigsaw puzzle in which the pieces are parts of the current curriculum that fit together to generate a complete picture. . . .
>
> The educators who wish to integrate curriculum are committed to a view of learning that sees all disciplines as interconnected and related to the life of the learner. They recognize that learning consists of searching for connections between the known and the new. (Bosma and Guth 1995, p. 1)

Students and researchers are urged to use their imaginations to find different ways of conceptualizing crime and justice issues. It is challenging but rewarding to engage in research from which one gleans relevant material from archival documents and produces work that is at the cutting edge of a discipline. Knowledge is everywhere if only we are willing to look for it. Perspectives of people in other disciplines increase the understanding of any issue. This broader understanding, as Shafer comments, proves the "validity of the interdisciplinary approach and suggests the degree of insight that could be attained through its use" (1976, p. 4). Finally, as Souryal advises, "Read philosophical literature and enjoy good books. . . . Refer them to your subordinates, colleagues, and superiors, so they might grow along with you" (1992, p. 371).

Appendix: Who Was William Shakespeare?

HIS EARLY LIFE

There is a consensus among Shakespearean scholars and writers that William Shakespeare was born in Stratford-on-Avon, England, to John and Mary Shakespeare (see Schoenbaum 1987; Neilson and Thorndike 1913; Elton 1904; Gareth and Evans 1978). The exact date and year of his birth are not recorded; however, because the inscription on his tombstone states that Shakespeare died on April 23, 1616, "*Aetatis* 53," Neilson and Thorndike suggest that this information, coupled with the fact that his baptism was registered in the church of the Holy Trinity in Stratford on April 26, 1564, indicates that the playwright must have been born at least as early as April 22 (1913, p. 18). They point out that, in those days, baptism usually took place within a few days of birth (pp. 18–19). According to Reese, in Shakespeare's time baptism was customarily performed a few days after the child's birth because of the high mortality rate among children (1964, p. 9). Because it was not customary to write biographies or autobiographies in Shakespeare's time (Neilson and Thorndike 1913, p. 17), specific events often went unrecorded. Schoenbaum notes that George Stevens, a prominent Shakespearean scholar, adopted April 23 as Shakespeare's birthday, and subsequent writers on Shakespeare have documented this date as the playwright's birthday (1987, p. 24). Schoenbaum suggests that we can assume that Shakespeare's birth occurred on April 21, 22, or 23, 1564.

It is speculated that because Stratford had a grammar school which was free for all children, Shakespeare probably attended that school (see Elton 1904; Rolfe 1904; Neilson and Thorndike 1913; Gareth and Evans 1978). As a prerequisite for admission into the school, children seven and above had to be able to read. Shakespeare probably learned to read (possibly at home) with the help of a hornbook or an A-B-C book (Rolf 1965, p. 44). Emphasis at the grammar school was placed on Latin and English, and *Lyly's Grammatica Latina* was a required text (Reese 1964; Rolfe 1965).

Churchgoing was obligatory in Stratford, and children were expected to recite their catechism; they were required to learn *Nowell's Catechism* in Latin at school (Schoenbaum 1987, p. 579). Shakespeare's training was geared toward the orthodox and Protestant religions.

Besides grammar, the students were taught logic, poetry, and history (1987, pp. 67–70). Schoenbaum makes the point that the grammar school in Stratford was an excellent institution; most of its teachers were graduates of Oxford University (p. 65). School hours were long, and classes were held six days a week, almost all year round (p. 67).

Reese portrays the poet as one who loved books but who did not particularly enjoy the laborious educational curriculum of his day (1964, p. 13). Whatever education Shakespeare received from the grammar school seems to be all the formal schooling he ever had (Rolfe 1965, p. 54). His talent was a natural endowment, and how he used it depended largely on external circumstances.

It is believed that sometime around 1577, Shakespeare's father, John, began to face severe financial decline, which eventually led to William Shakespeare's withdrawal from school in order to help out in his father's business (Schoenbaum 1987, p. 73; Neilson and Thorndike 1913, p. 19; Rolfe 1965, p. 77). Some writers suggest that Shakespeare worked as a lawyer's clerk when he left the grammar school (Gareth and Evans 1978; Finkelstein 1973). There is however no proof of this (Rolfe 1904, p. 77). Reese documents a variety of trades Shakespeare is alleged to have held: an apprentice butcher, a schoolmaster in the country, a clerk, a seaman, a soldier, a singing boy, and a companion and tutor in a noble man's household (1964, pp. 26–27). These are all mere conjectures.

Although there are no actual marriage records, it is believed that Shakespeare married Anne Hathaway, a lady eight years older than the Bard (Halliday 1962, p. 42; Neilson and Thorndike 1913; Elton 1904). Together they had three children (Neilson and Thorndike 1913, p. 20).

It has also been conjectured that Shakespeare was once charged with theft of a deer at the Lucy farm (Gareth and Evans 1978; Elton 1904; Reese 1964). However, as pointed out by these authors, there is no evidence that substantiates the allegation. Elton calls the allegations an "invention" (1904, p. 38).

HIS PROFESSIONAL LIFE

Sometime around 1586 Shakespeare moved to London where his career in theater began (Elton 1904; Neilson and Thorndike 1913). According to Neilson and Thorndike, Shakespeare's career allegedly began as a "call-boy" or as "holder of the horses of theatergoers" 1913, p. 20). As a horse boy, Shakespeare received the necessary exposure to those who frequented the theaters. In time, he was to blend his experiences with his natural talents to become one of the greatest playwrights of all time. According to Rolfe, for seven years while Shakespeare was in London (1585–1592), no information concerning the poet is recorded (1904, p. 146).

By about 1592, Shakespeare had done well enough to arouse the jealousy of other playwrights, especially Robert Greene (Martin 1965, p. 20; Neilson and Thorndike 1913, p. 20). Greene published *Groatsworth of Wit* (1592), in which he referred to Shakespeare as "the upstart Crow" and expressed contempt for him (Martin 1965, p. 20; Neilson and Thorndike 1913, pp. 20–22).

Shakespeare seems to have begun his career as a playwright in 1590, with *2 Henry VI*, but he did not make his breakthrough in the literary world until 1593 when he published his poem *Venus and Adonis* (Neilson and Thorndike 1913, p. 23; Martin 1965, p. 20; Halliwell-Phillipps 1966, p. 70). Shakespeare's interest in theater was not limited to writing alone; he also engaged in acting (Elton 1904; Neilson and Thorndike 1913). In all, the playwright is credited with the authorship of thirty-seven plays and a series of poems.

Death of Shakespeare

There are conflicting accounts of the causes of Shakespeare's death. It is certain that the playwright died in 1616. Unconfirmed entries have been reported about Shakespeare's death in a diary that belonged to John Ward, the vicar of Stratford from 1662 to 1681 (Gareth and Evans 1978, p. 22; Reese, 1964). According to notes in that diary, "Shakespeare, Drayton, and Ben Johnson had a meeting, and it seems drank too hard, for Shakespeare died of a fever there contracted." Elton also mentions John Ward's account (1904, pp. 306–7) but would rather consider the bard's death to have been caused by what Dr. Stevens called, in his own edition of the vicar's diary, "low typhoid fever" (Schoenbaum 1987, p. 296; Elton 1904, p. 230).

HIS WORKS

There are conflicting accounts of the dates on which Shakespeare first published his plays. This study has used the ordering of the plays sug-

gested by D. Bevington (1980), which is the most cogent and widely
accepted chronology today.

Plays

1589–1593	*The Comedy of Errors*
1588–1589 Rev. 1596–97(?)	*Love's Labour's Lost*
1590–1594	*The Two Gentlemen of Verona*
1589–1591	*Titus Andronicus*
1589–1592	*1 Henry VI*
1589–1592	*2 Henry VI*
1589–1592	*3 Henry VI*
1591–1594	*Richard III*
1592–1594	*The Taming of the Shrew*
1594–1595	*A Midsummer Night's Dream*
1594–1596	*Romeo and Juliet*
1594–1592	*King John*
1595–1596	*Richard II*
1594–1598	*The Merchant of Venice*
1596–1598	*1 Henry IV*
1596–1598	*2 Henry IV*
1598–1599	*Much Ado About Nothing*
1598–1600	*As You Like It*
1599	*Henry V*
1599	*Julius Caesar*
1597–1601	*The Merry Wives of Windsor*
1600–1602	*Twelfth Night*
1599–1601	*Hamlet*
1601–1602	*Troilus and Cressida*
1601–1604	*All's Well That Ends Well*
1603–1604	*Measure for Measure*
1603–1604	*Othello*
1605	*King Lear*
1605–1608	*Timon of Athens*
1606–1607	*Macbeth*
1606–1607	*Antony and Cleopatra*
1606–1608	*Pericles*

1608	*Coriolanus*
1608–1610	*Cymberline*
1610–1611	*The Winter's Tale*
1610–1611	*The Tempest*
1613	*Henry VIII*

Poems

1592–1593	*Venus and Adonis*
1593–1594	*The Rape of Lucrece*
1595–1599	*Sonnets*
1595–1599	*A Lover's Complaint*
1599	*The Passionate Pilgrim*
1600	"The Phoenix and Turtle"

SYNOPSIS OF PLAYS IN THE SAMPLE

The Merchant of Venice

This play tells the story about a wealthy usurer, Shylock, from whom Antonio, a merchant, borrows money to enable his friend Bassanio to secure his lover's consent for marriage. Antonio had no money at the time, but because he was expecting a shipload of merchandise, he decided to borrow money from Shylock. Antonio asked Shylock to lend him 3,000 ducats, hoping to refund the money with interest upon the sale of his merchandise.

Shylock lends Antonio the money on the proviso that, if Antonio does not repay the money by a certain day, he will forfeit a pound of flesh to be cut off from any part of his body: "[I]f you repay me not on such a day, in such a place, such sum or sums as are express'd in the condition, let the forfeit be nominated for an equal pound of your fair flesh, to be cut off and taken in what part of your body pleaseth me" (I.iii.153–158).

When he is unable to repay Shylock the money on the due date, Antonio is taken to court. He is represented by a young lawyer, who at the end of the play is revealed to be Portia, Bassanio's bethrothed. The court entreats Shylock to withdaw the case or to take from Antonio money three times more than the debt. Shylock declines the offer and insists on the execution of the terms of the bond. The young lawyer pleads with Shylock to be merciful because he who shows mercy gets mercy in return: "[T]he quality of mercy is not strain'd, it droppeth as the gentle rain from heaven upon the place beneath: it is twice blest; it blesseth him that gives and him that takes" (IV.i.203–6). Shylock remains intransigent, whereupon the young lawyer grants Shylock his wish on the condition that he cut no less or no more of the flesh and shed no drop of Antonio's blood.

This being impossible, Shylock agrees to take the original offer of money. The young lawyer declines this gesture as coming too late. Shylock is ordered to forfeit his wealth to the state for conspiring against the life of one of its citizens. Part of the wealth was then issued to Antonio who declined it but requested that it be willed to Shylock's daughter.

Measure for Measure

In this play, the Duke temporarily relinquishes his responsibilities to his deputy, Angelo, and then dresses in disguise as a friar to listen to the problems of the state.

The laws of Vienna were very strict, but for several years, because of the Duke's ineptitude, his subjects had broken the laws with impunity. The law against fornication sentenced violators to death, but because it was not enforced, no one was deterred. When the Duke sees the morals of his subjects degenerate, he temporarily abdicates his throne in order that his strict and well-reputed deputy restore law and order in the state.

Angelo immediately sets out to enforce the law which he states "hath not been dead, though it hath slept" (II.ii.120–21). It is brought to Angelo's attention that Claudio has violated the law by seducing his fiancée. Angelo will not consider any mitigating circumstances in Claudio's case because "we must not make a scarecrow of the law, setting it up to fear the birds of prey, and let it keep one shape till custom make it their perch, and not their terror" (II.i.1–5). Claudio must die. Claudio entreats his sister, Isabella, a nun, to intercede on his behalf, but Angelo will not concede unless Isabella goes to bed with him.

The Duke, posing as a friar, concocts a plan. He disguises Mariana, Angelo's estranged betrothed, as Isabella, who gives in to Angelo's request. The plan works. Angelo, who has insisted on executing Claudio, is now guilty of the same offense. Although he gracefully asks that the same punishment be meted out to him, the Duke, who now "returns" to reclaim his throne, pardons him and lets him marry Mariana. Claudio is also pardoned and ordered to marry Juliet, his fiancée. Other criminals who had been sentenced under the harsh laws had their cases reviewed, and punishments proportionate to the crimes were imposed on the wrongdoers.

Othello

Brabantio, a senator of Venice, has a daughter called Desdemona, who has many wealthy suitors but chooses Othello, a black Moor, for her husband. Othello, a brave and hard-working soldier, had risen to the rank of general in the Venetian army. The marriage was secretly contracted. When Brabantio found out, he was enraged that his daughter had rejected so many worthy white suitors for a Moor. Brabantio later recanted and approved the marriage.

Because Venice was being threatened by a Turkish invasion off the coast of Cyprus, Othello's services were needed. Othello and his bride leave for Cyprus, but upon arrival, they hear that their foes have been dispersed by a storm.

Othello, as general, promoted Cassio, a serviceman, to position of lieutenant. This gesture apparently offended Iago, who had hoped to receive that favor instead. This slight, coupled with an unfounded perception that Othello was too fond of Emilia, Iago's wife, generated in Iago a scheme of evil deeds. His first act of revenge was to cause Cassio's dismissal from his position as lieutenant. He then turned Othello's mind against his wife, Desdemona, by making him believe that she was unfaithful to him. Outraged by this, Othello kills Desdemona: "[Y]et she must die, else she'll betray more men" (V.ii.6).

Macbeth

Duncan, the king of Scotland, had a competent general called Macbeth. One day, Macbeth was approached by three witches whose greetings, "[A]ll hail! King thou shall be here after!" suggest to Macbeth that he is destined to become king. Macbeth apprises his wife, Lady Macbeth, of the witches' prophesy. An ambitious woman, Lady Macbeth plans to see the witches' prediction fulfilled at once.

As was his practice, the king made visits to his generals to congratulate them for their valor. Such a visit was planned to Macbeth's home. Lady Macbeth regards this visit as the perfect opportunity to get rid of the king so that Macbeth can become king in his stead.

Late that night, Lady Macbeth plots the murder of the king. Knowing that her husband lacks the resoluteness to murder Duncan, she decides to commit the murder herself. While the king and the guards are sleeping, Lady Macbeth arms herself with a dagger and approaches the king's bed. She cannot commit the murder, however, because "had he not resembled my father as he slept, I had done't" (II.i.86–87). Lady Macbeth thereafter urges her husband to do it, and he eventually succumbs to the pressure and carries out the murder. Attempts at covering up the crime are unsuccessful. The Macbeths continue in their criminal pursuits. At the end, Lady Macbeth apparently dies at her own hands, and Macbeth dies at the hands of Macduff.

Richard III

Richard, Duke of Gloster, became king of England after committing treason and a series of murders. Richard was badly deformed from birth: "I that am curtailed of this fair proportion, cheated of feature by dissembling nature, deform'd, unfinished . . . so lamely and unfashionable that dogs bark at me" (I.i.21–23, 25–26). As a result, he was full of jealousy, self-pity, and hatred.

From an early age, Richard set his mind on the crown. Although badly deformed, he had enormous energy and great resolve. He knew he had claims to the crown, but "many lives stand between me and home" (*3 Henry VI*, III.ii.231). Therefore, he is "determined to prove a villain" (*Richard III*, I.i.34) and to wear the crown by any means. He kills Edward, Prince of Wales, and his father, King Henry VI. He then convinces Edward's widow to marry him because it is "the readiest way to make the wench amends" (I.i.187), although he "will have her; but will not keep her long" (I.ii.246). His next victim is Clarence. Through acts of violence, Richard gets rid of everyone who stands between him and the throne while the people "spake not a word" (III.vii.26).

Richard eventually becomes king, but then he realizes that even as king he cannot restrain himself from killing. He knows that for as much crime as he has committed "there is no creature loves me; and if I die, no soul shall pity me: nay, wherefore should they,—since that I myself find in myself no pity to myself?" (V.iii.242–45). Richard meets his death at the hands of Richmond at the field of Bosworth.

1 Henry IV

This play has two main plots. First, Henry Percy, alias Hotspur, and the rest of the Percy allies challenge the legitimacy of King Henry IV to the English throne. Second, Prince Hal (the son of King Henry) abandons the lifestyle of royalty for a wild and irresponsible lifestyle with Falstaff.

Because King Henry IV had obtained the crown of England by usurpation, the Percys and their allies, led by Hotspur, were fighting against the king to reclaim the throne. At the same time, Prince Hal, who was about the same age as Hotspur, had distanced himself from his father, leaving his father to wish "that some night-tripping fairy had exchang'd in cradle-clothes (their) children where they lay, and called his Percy his Plantagenet!" (I.i.100–103).

Prince Hal, Falstaff, and their cronies meanwhile engaged in loose living, hanging around bars, and robbing. Prince Hal plans to redeem himself "at a time when men think least" (I.ii.244) he would; and he vows to his father that he "will redeem all this on Percy's head" (III.ii.144), and at "some glorious day . . . wear a garment all of blood" (III.ii.145, 147). Hal makes true his vow at the end of the play when he challenges Hotspur to a fight and kills him.

Bibliography

Adler, F., G. Mueller, and W. Laufer. (1995). *Criminology*. 2d ed. New York: McGraw-Hill.
———. (1998). *Criminology*. 3d ed. New York: McGraw-Hill.
Akers, R. (1994). *Criminological Theories*. Los Angeles: Roxbury Publishing.
———. (1997). *Criminological Theories*. 2d ed. Los Angeles: Roxbury Publishing.
Alvis, J., and R. West. (1981). *Shakespeare as a Political Thinker*. Durham, N.C.: Carolina Academic Press.
Andenaes, J. (1974). *Punishment and Deterrence*. Ann Arbor: University of Michigan Press.
Anderson, L. M. (1985). "A Kind of Wild Justice: Revenge as Theme and Device in Shakespeare's Comedies." Ph.D. diss., Abstract in *Dissertation Abstracts International*.
Andrews, M. E. (1969). *Laws Versus Equity in* The Merchant of Venice. Boulder: University of Colorado Press.
The Annals of the American Academy of Political and Social Science. (1982). Vol. 462. Beverly Hills & London: Sage Publishing.
Bailey, W., and R. Peterson. (1994). "Murder, Capital Punishment and Deterrence: A Review of the Evidence and an Examination of Police Killings." *Journal of Social Issues* 50: 53–74.
Ball, J. (1955). "The Deterrent Concept in Criminology and the Law." *Journal of Criminal Law, Criminology, and Police Science* 46: 349–54.
Bartol, C. (1980). *Criminal Behavior*. Englewood Cliffs, N.J.: Prentice Hall.

————. (1991). *Criminal Behavior*. 3d ed. Englewood Cliffs, N.J.: Prentice Hall.

Bawcutt, N. W. (1984). "He Who the Sword of Heaven Will Bear: The Duke Versus Angelo in *Measure for Measure.*" *Shakespeare Survey* 37: 89–97.

Baydallaye, K. (1988). "Quelques aspects des fondements philosophiques de l'exercice de la peine de mort dans le théâtre de Shakespeare." In *Société Française Shakespeare, Actes du Congrès*, edited by Jean-François Gournay, 88–106. Paris: Touzot.

Beccaria, C. (1963). *On Crimes and Punishments*. (1809). Translated with an introduction by Henry Paolucci. New York: Macmillan Publishing.

Becker, H. (1963). *Outsiders: Studies in the Sociology of Deviance*. New York: Free Press.

Bedau, H. (1967). *The Death Penalty in America*. Garden City, N.Y.: Anchor Books.

————. (1970). "The Death Penalty as a Deterrent: Argument and Evidence." *Ethics* 80: 205–17.

————. (1982). *The Death Penalty in America*. 3d ed. New York: Oxford University Press.

————. (1997) *The Death Penalty in America: Current Controversies*. New York: Oxford University Press.

Beier, A. L. (1985). *Masterless Men*. London: Methuen.

Bernard, T. J. (1990). "Twenty Years of Testing Theories: What Have We Learned and Why?" *Journal of Research in Crime and Delinquency* 27, no. 4: 325–47.

Bevington, D. (1980). *The Complete Works of Shakespeare*. 3d ed. Glenview, Ill.: Scott, Foresman.

Black, D. (1972). *The Behavior of Law*. New York: Academic Press.

Black, H. (1990). *Black's Law Dictionary*. St. Paul: West Publishing.

Blumstein, A., J. Cohen, and D. Nagin. (1980). *Deterrence & Incapacitation: Estimating the Effects of Criminal Sanctions on Crime Rates*. Washington, D.C.: National Academy of Science.

Bosma, B., and D. Guth. (1995). *Children's Literature in an Integrated Curriculum*. New York: Teachers College Press.

Bourgy, V. (1988). "La fin et les moyens: Le juste et le tout juste dans quelques denouements Shakespeariens." In *Société Française Shakespeare, Actes du Congrès*, edited by Jean-François Gournay, 65–87. Paris: Touzot.

Brown, J. R. (1982). *Focus on Macbeth*. London: Routledge & Keegan Paul.

Campbell, S. (1992). "Is That the Law?: Shakespeare's Political Cynicism in *The Merchant of Venice.*" *Cookson Longman Critical Essays* 3, no. 2: 65–74.

Caspi, Avshalom, T. Moffit, et al. (1994). "Are Some People Crime-prone?

Replications of the Personality—Crime Relationship across Coun-
   tries, Genders, Races, and Methods." *Criminology* 32: 163–96.
Champion, D. (1997). *Research Methods for Criminal Justice and Criminology*.
   Englewood Cliffs, N.J.: Regents/Prentice Hall.
Clark, W. and W. Wright. (1864). *Shakespeare, Complete Works* (n.p.).
Cloward, R., and L. Ohlin (1960). *Delinquency and Opportunity*. Glencoe,
   Ill.: Free Press.
Cohen, D. (1993). *Shakespeare's Culture of Violence*. New York: St. Martin's
   Press.
The Complete Works of Shakespeare. (n.d.). Edited by W. Black. New York:
   Walter J. Black.
Conway D. (1985). "Capital Punishment and Deterrence: Some Consid-
   erations in Dialogue Form." In *Punishment and Rehabilitation*, ed-
   ited by J. Murphy. Belmont, Calif.: Wadsworth Publishing.
Cullen, F., and R. Agnew. (1999). *Criminological Theory Past to Present*. Los
   Angeles: Roxbury Publishing.
Curran, D., and C. Renzetti. (1994). *Theories of Crime*. Boston: Allyn and
   Bacon.
Denno, D. (1985). "Sociological and Human Developmental Explanations
   of Crime: Conflict or Consensus." *Criminology* 23, no. 4: 235–52.
Deviant Behavior: An Interdisciplinary Journal. (1980). Vol. 2: 1–13. Hemi-
   sphere Publishing.
Dostoevsky, F. (1956). *Crime and Punishment*. New York: Random House.
Draper, J. (1961). *Stratford to Dogberry*. Pittsburgh: University of Pitts-
   burgh Press.
Dugdale, R. (1910). *The Jukes*. New York: Putnam.
Durkheim, E. (1951). *Suicide*. (1897). Translated by John A. Spaulding and
   George Simpson. New York: Free Press.
———. (1964). *The Division of Labor in Society*. New York: Free Press.
Edgerton, R. B. (1976). *Deviance: A Cross-Cultural Perspective*. London:
   Cummings Publishing.
Ehrlich, I. (1973). "The Deterrent Effect of Capital Punishment: A Ques-
   tion of Life or Death." Working Paper No. 18, National Bureau of
   Economic Research, November.
———. (1975). "The Deterrent Effect of Capital Punishment: A Question
   of Life and Death." *American Economic Review* 65: 397.
Eldridge, W. B. (1982). "Shifting Views of the Sentencing Function." *An-
   nals of the American Academy of Political and Social Sciences* (July):
   108.
Elliot, D. (1985). "The Assumption That Theories Can Be Combined with
   Increased Explanatory Power." In *Theoretical Methods in Criminol-
   ogy*, edited by Robert F. Meier, 123–49. Beverly Hills, Calif: Sage.
Elton, C. I. (1904). *William Shakespeare, His Family and Friends*, edited by
   Thomas A. Hamilton. London: Cassell and Company.

Fello, S. (1992). "A Content Analysis of the AIDS Health Curricula Used in Elementary Schools Within the Commonwealth of Pennsylvania." Ph.D. diss., University of Pennsylvania.

Ferracuti, F., and M. Wolfgang. (1963). "Criminology and the Criminologist." *Journal of Criminal Law, Criminology and Police Science* 54, no. 2: 156–58.

Finkelstein, S. (1973). *Who Needs Shakespeare?* New York: International Publishers.

Fishbein, D. (1990). "Biological Perspectives in Criminology." *Criminology* 28: 27–72.

Friedman, L. (1984). *American Law*. New York & London: W. W. Norton.

Gareth, A., and B. Evans. (1978). *Everyman's Companion to Shakespeare*. New York: Charles Scribner & Sons.

Garland, D. (1990). *Punishment and Modern Society: A Study in Social Theory*. Chicago: University of Chicago Press.

Garland, D. (1991). "Punishment and Culture: The Symbolic Dimension of Criminal Justice. *Studies in Law, Politics, and Society* 11: 191–222.

Gibbs, J. P. (1975). *Crime, Punishment, and Deterrence*. New York: Elsevier.

Gifis, S. (1984). *Law Dictionary*. New York, London, Toronto, Sydney, Woodbury: Barron's Educational Series, Inc.

Glaser, B., and A. Strauss. (1967). *The Discovery of Grounded Theory: Strategies for Qualitative Research*. Chicago: Aldine de Gruyer.

Gless, D. (1979). *Measure for Measure, the Law, and the Covenant*. Princeton, N.J.: Princeton University Press.

Goddard, H. (1927). *The Kallikak Family: A Study in the Heredity of Feeble-Mindedness*. New York: MacMillan.

Goldman, S. (1982). "Judicial Selection and the Qualities That Make a 'Good' Judge." *The Annals of the American Academy of Political and Social Science* (1982): 112–24.

Goll, A. (1966). *Criminal Types in Shakespeare*. (1909). Translated from the Danish by Mrs. Charles Weeks. New York: Haskel House.

Gottfredson, M., and T. Hirschi. (1990). *A General Theory of Crime*. Stanford, CA: Stanford University Press.

Halio, J. L. (1993). "Portia: Shakespeare's Matlock?" *Cardozo Studies in Law and Literature* 5 (Spring): 1.1.

Halliday, F. E. (1962). *Shakespeare*. New York: Thomas Yoseloff.

Halliwell-Phillipps, J. O. (1966). *Outlines of the Life of Shakespeare*. New York: AMS Press.

Hare, R. (1970). *Psychopathy: Theory and Research*. New York: Wiley.

Hart, H. (1968). *Punishment and Responsibility*. Oxford: Oxford University Press.

Hirschi, T. (1969). *Causes of Delinquency*. Berkeley: University of California Press.

———. (1979). "Separate and Unequal Is Better," *Journal of Research in Crime and Delinquency* 16: 34–38.

The Holy Bible. (1961). Authorized (King James) Version. Chicago: National Publishing.

Honderich, T. (1971). *Punishment, the Supposed Justification*. Harmonds-
worth: Pelican Books.

Hood, O. P. (1964). "The Law Relating to Shakespeare." *Law Quarterly
Review* 80: 20–32.

Inbau, F., et al. (1997). *Criminal Law & Its Administration*. Westbury,
Conn.: Foundation Press.

Jeffrey, C. R. (1965). "Criminal Behavior and Learning Theory." *Journal
of Criminal Law, Criminology, and Police Science* 56: 294–300.

————. (1978). "Criminology as an Interdisciplinary Behavioral Science."
Criminology 16, no. 2: 149–69.

Katz, J., and W. Chambliss. (1995). "Biology and Crime." In *Criminology:
A Contemporary Handbook*, 2d ed., edited by Joseph F. Sheley, 275–
303. Belmont, Calif.: Wadsworth.

Keeton, G. W. (1967). *Shakespeare's Legal and Political Background*. New
York: Barnes and Noble.

Knight, C. (1971). *William Shakespeare: A Biography*. New York: AMS
Press.

Knight, W. G. (1967). *Shakespeare and Religion*. London: Routledge and
Kegan Paul.

Knights, L. C. (1957). "Shakespeare's Politics: With Some Reflections on
the Nature of Tradition." *Proceedings of the British Academy* 43: 115–
32.

Kockelmans, J. J. (1979). *Interdisciplinarity and Higher Education*. Philadelphia: Pennsylvania State University Press.

Koessler, M. (1964). *Masterpieces of Legal Fiction*. Rochester, N.Y.: Lawyers
Co-operative Publishing Company.

Layson, S. (1985). "Homicide and Deterrence: An Examination of the
United States Time-Series Evidence." *Southern Economic Journal* 52:
68–89.

Leggatt, A. (1988). *Shakespeare's Political Drama*. London & New York:
Routledge Publishing.

Lemert, E. (1951). *Social Pathology*. New York: McGraw-Hill.

Lyman, W. (1956). *Reflections of the Law in Literature*. Philadelphia: University of Pennsylvania Press.

Makaryk, I. R. (1980). "Comic Justice in Shakespeare's Comedies." Insti-
tut für Anglistik und Amerikanistik, Universitat Salzburg.

Mannheim, H. (1967). *Comparative Criminology*. Boston: Houghton Mifflin.

Martin, M. (1965). *Was Shakespeare Shakespeare? A Lawyer Reviews the Evidence*. New York: Cooper Square Publishers.

Martin, R., R. Mutchnick, and T. Austin (1990). *Criminological Thought*.
New York: Macmillan.

Mednick, S. (1977). "A Biosocial Theory of the Learning of Law Abiding
Behavior." In *Biosocial Bases of Criminal Behavior*, edited by S. Mednick and K. Christensen, 1–8. New York: Gardner.

Mehl, D. (1986). "Corruption, Retribution and Justice in *Measure for Measure* and the *Revenger's Tragedy*." In *Shakespeare and His Contemporaries: Essays in Comparison*, edited by E. A. Honigman, 114–28. Manchester, England: Manchester University Press.

Menninger, K. (1985). "Therapy, Not Punishment." In *Punishment and Rehabilitation*, edited by J. Murphy, 175–89. Belmont, Calif: Wadsworth Publishing.

Merton, R. (1938). "Social Structure and Anomie." *American Sociological Review* 3: 672–82.

Merton, R. K. (1957). *Social Theory and Social Structure*. Glencoe, Ill.: Free Press.

Milward, P. (1987). *Biblical Influences in Shakespeare's Great Tragedies*. Indianapolis: Indiana University Press.

Model Penal Code and Commentaries (1980). Vol. 2. Philadelphia: American Law Institute.

Moffitt, T. E. (1993). "Adolescent-Limited and Life Course Persistent Antisocial Behavior: A Developmental Taxonomy." *Psychological Review* 100: 674–701.

———. (1997). "Adolescent-Limited and Life Course Persistent Offending: A Complementary Pair of Developmental Theories." In *Developmental Theories of Crime and Delinquency, Advances in Criminological Theory*, vol. 7, edited by T. Thornberry. New Brunswick, N.J.: Transaction.

Morris, C. (1953). *Political Thought in England: Tyndale to Hooker*, 103. London & New York: Oxford University Press.

Mourad, R. P. (1997). *Postmodern Philosophical Critique and the Pursuit of Knowledge in Higher Education*. Westport, Conn.: Bergin & Garvey.

Murphy, J. (1985). *Punishment and Rehabilitation*. Belmont, Calif: Wadsworth Publishing.

Murphy, J. G., J. and Hampton. (1990). *Forgiveness and Mercy*. Cambridge, England: Cambridge University Press.

Neilson, W., and A. Thorndike. (1913). *The Facts About Shakespeare*. New York: Macmillan.

Ogburn, W. F. (1952). *Social Change*. 2d ed. New York: Viking Press.

Park, R. E., and E. W. Burgess. (1924). *Introduction to the Science of Sociology*. Chicago: University of Chicago Press.

———. (1925). *The City*. Chicago: University of Chicago Press.

Phelps, C. (1901). *Falstaff and Equity*. New York: Houghton, Mifflin.

Pories, K. G. (1995). "Fashioning the Face of Poverty in Early Modern England (Criminals, Idle Poor)." Ph.D. diss., University of North Carolina, Chapel Hill.

President's Commission on Law Enforcement and Administration of Justice. (1967). *Challenge of Crime in a Free Society*. Washington, D.C.: U.S. Government Printing Office.

Quinney, R. (1970). *The Social Reality of Crime*. Boston: Little, Brown.
———. (1980). *Class, State, and Crime*. 2d ed. New York: Longman.
Radin, M. J. (1985) "Cruel Punishment and Respect for Persons: Super Due Process for Death." In *Punishment and Rehabilitation*, edited by J. Murphy, 134–68. Belmont, Calif.: Wadsworth Publishing.
Raine, A. (1994). "Diminished Capacity Examined: Experts Give Support to View That the Criminal Mind Is Different." *St. Louis Post-Dispatch*, July 26, 1994, p. 1.
Rawls, J. (1985). "Punishment as Practice." In *Punishment and Rehabilitation*, edited by J. Murphy, 68–73. Belmont, Calif.: Wadsworth Publishing.
Reed, R. (1984). *Crime and God's Judgment in Shakespeare*. Lexington: University of Kentucky Press.
Reese, M. M. (1964). *Shakespeare, His World and His Work*. London: Edward Arnold Publishers.
Reid, S. T. (1997). *Crime and Criminology*. 8th ed. Madison, Wisc.: Brown & Benchmark Publishing.
Rolfe, W. J. (1904). *A Life of William Shakespeare*. Boston: Dana Estes Publishers.
———. (1965). *Shakespeare the Boy*. New York: Frederick Ungar Publishing.
Rouseau, M. (1981). "Du Richard III de nore a celui de Shakespeare: Deux regards Sur justice et pouvoir." *Societe Française Shakespeare, Actes du Congres*. Paris: Jean Touzot Libraire.
Rush, G. (1986). *The Dictionary of Criminal Justice*. Guilford, Conn.: Dushkin Publishing.
Sagarin, E. (1980). "In Search of Criminology through Fiction." *Deviant Behavior* 2, no. 1.
Salgado, G. (1977). *The Elizabethan Underworld*. London: Rowman & Littlefield.
Samaha, J. (1996). *Criminal Law*. 5th ed. Minneapolis/St. Paul: West.
———. (1997). *Criminal Justice*. 5th ed. Belmont, Calif.: West.
———. (1999). *Criminal Law*. 6th ed. Belmont, Calif.: West.
Sampson, R. (1986). "Crime in Cities: The Effects of Formal and Informal Social Control." In *Communities and Crime*, edited by A. Reiss and M. Tonry, 271–311. Chicago: University of Chicago Press.
Schafer, S. (1969). *Theories in Criminology*. New York: Random House.
———. (1976). *Introduction to Criminology*. Reston, VA: Reston Publishing.
Schoenbaum, S. (1987). *William Shakespeare: A Compact Documentary Life*. New York: Oxford University Press.
Sellin, T. (1980). *The Penalty of Death*. Beverly Hills, Calif.: Sage Publications.
Sexton, G. (1869). *The Psychology of Macbeth*. New York: AMS Press.
Shafer, R. (1976). Introduction to a lecture series titled *Shakespeare and*

English History: Interdisciplinary Perspectives. Indiana: Indiana University of Pennsylvania Press.

Sharpe, J. A. (1984). *Crime in Early Modern England, 1550–1750*. London & New York: Longman.

Shaw, C. (1951). *The Natural History of a Delinquent Career*. Philadelphia: Saifer.

Shaw, C., and H. McKay. (1969). *Juvenile Delinquency and Urban Areas*. Rev. ed. Chicago: University of Chicago Press.

Siegel, L. (1983). *Criminology*. Belmont, Calif.: West.

Sigler, J. (1981). *Understanding Criminal Law*. Boston & Toronto: Little, Brown.

Souryal, S. (1992). *Ethics in Criminal Justice*. Cincinnati: Anderson Publishing.

Spinosa, C. D. (1993). "Shakespeare and Common-law Understanding." Ph.D. diss. abstract in *Dissertation Abstracts International*.

Stokes, M. (1984). *Justice and Mercy in Piers Plowman*. London: Croom Helm.

Sutherland, E. (1947). *Principles of Criminology*. 4th ed. Philadelphia: J. B. Lippincott.

Sutherland, E. H., D. R. Cressey, and D. Linkenbill. (1992). *Principles of Criminology*. 11th ed. Dix Hills, N.Y.: General Hall.

Sykes, A., and D. Matza. (1957). "Techniques of Neutralization: A Theory of Delinquency." *American Journal of Sociology* 22: 664–70.

Tannenbaum, F. (1938). *Crime and the Community*. New York: Columbia University Press.

Theodorson, G. A., and A. G. Theodorson. (1969). *Modern Dictionary of Sociology*. New York: Thomas Y. Crowell.

Thilly, F. (1914). *History of Philosophy*. London: Henry Holt.

Thornberry, T. (1996). "Empirical Support for Interactional Theory." In *Delinquency and Crime: Current Theories*, edited by J. David Hawkins, pp. 198–235. Cambridge: Cambridge University Press.

Thornberry, T. P. (1987). "Toward an Interactional Theory of Delinquency." *Criminology* 25: 863–91.

Tonnies, F. (1957). *Community and Society*. (1887). Translated and edited by Charles P. Loomis. East Lansing: Michigan State University Press.

Triplett, R., and R. Jarjoura. (1994). "Theoretical and Empirical Specification of a Model of Informal Labeling." *Journal of Quantitative Criminology* 10: 241–76.

Vold, G. (1979). *Theoretical Criminology*, 2d ed. New York: Oxford University Press.

Vold, G., and T. Bernard. (1986). *Theoretical Criminology*. 3d ed. New York: Oxford University Press.

von Hirsch, A. (1976). *Doing Justice: The Choice of Punishments*. New York: Hill and Wang.

Walker, N. (1991). *Why Punish?* New York: Oxford University Press.

Wallace, W. (1971). *The Logic of Science in Sociology*. Chicago: Aldine-Atherton.

Wasserstrom, R. (1985). "Problems with the Therapeutic Approach to Criminality." In *Punishment and Rehabilitation*, edited by J. Murphy, 190–97. Belmont, Calif.: Wadsworth.

White, R. S. (1986). *Innocent Victims: Poetic Justice in Shakespeare Tragedy*. London: Athlone Press.

Widmayer, M. (1988). "The Great 'Fever of Goodness': 'Measure for Measure' and the War over Reform." Ph.D. diss., University of Miami.

Williams, C. (1963). *A Short Life of Shakespeare with the Sources*. Abridged from Sir Edmund Chamber's Oxford. Oxford: Clarendon Press.

Williams, F. and M. McShane. (1988). *Criminological Theory*. Englewood Cliffs, N.J.: Prentice Hall.

Wilson, R. (1990). "The Quality of Mercy: Discipline and Punishment in Shakespearean Comedy." *Seventeenth Century* 5 (Spring): 1.

Wolfgang, C. (1968). *A Commentary on Shakespeare's Richard III*. New York: Methuen Publishers.

Wolfgang, M., and F. Ferracuti. (1982). *The Subculture of Violence*. Beverly Hills, Calif.: Sage.

Zimring, F., and G. Hawkins. (1973). *Deterrence: The Legal Threat in Crime Control*. Chicago: University of Chicago Press.

———. (1986). *Capital Punishment and the American Agenda*. New York: Cambridge University Press.

Zuckert, C. (1996). "Why Political Scientists Study Fiction." *Chronicle of Higher Education* 42, no. 26: A48.

Index

About the Author

VICTORIA M. TIME is Assistant Professor of Criminal Justice at Old Dominion University.